HUMBLY SUBMITTING TO CHANGE

THE WILDERNESS EXPERIENCE

E'YEN A. GARDNER

HUMBLY SUBMITTING TO CHANGE
Copyright © 2008 by E'yen A. Gardner

Printed Word Publishing
PO BOX 360812
Columbus, Ohio 43236

PH: 614-678-5353
FAX: 888-221-3166

www.pwpublish.com
contact@pwpublish.com

Printed in the United States of America

All Scripture bible references are from the King James Version of the Holy Bible.

All rights reserved. No part of this book may be reproduced or transmitted in any form or by any means without written permission of the author.

Book Editing: Maia R. Gardner, Senior Editor

Cover Design: Katawi K. Cato, Graphic Designer
                www.kcatodesign.com
                katawicato@gmail.com

ISBN: 978-0-615294-02-5
Library of Congress Control Number: 2009904122

Acknowledgements

I must thank my Lord and God Jesus Christ for choosing to use me to share His words to the world. Your love is amazing and this book is yours. You get all the glory and honor through the words that will empower a generation to seek a more intimate relationship with You. Thank you for the wilderness experience, for through it I have learned who I am and who You are. Thank You for taking the time to mold me for Your service.

Without the amazing efforts of my wife Maia this book would not have been possible. You are the strongest person that I know. Your strength has inspired me to go after the call of God. I am a better man for my connection to such a beautiful and anointed woman of God. Thank you for your prayers, encouragement, editing, and love.

To my children Arin, J'sun, Raya, Lesa, and Kyan and any other children with whom the Lord has yet to bless us with, thank you for being the best children in the world. I can see greatness in each one of you and "Dada" loves you. Each one of you has made me a better person and servant of God.

Thank you Katawi for your gracious efforts in creating the book cover design.

To my Eliezer Church Family thank you for your prayers, your love and encouragement.

Contents

Preface	pg. 7
Introduction	pg. 11
The Wilderness	pg. 15
Supply in Drought	pg. 21
Comfort in a Dry Place	pg. 31
Built to Last	pg. 39
Alone with God	pg. 49
Following the Pillar	pg. 61
The Wisdom of God	pg. 71
Becoming a Deliverer	pg. 79
Validated by Purpose	pg. 91
Finding Faith	pg. 101
An Empty Bottle	pg. 117
Submitting to Change	pg. 129
Loving God	pg. 143
God's Heart	pg. 159
God's Eyes	pg. 169
God's Life	pg. 183
A Life of Ministry	pg. 191

Preface

In life we come to many crossroads but there is only one path that leads to the Presence of God. Are we willing to take a journey to understanding our life's purpose? Or will we continue to pursue God on our own terms?

God is calling us to journey into the wilderness. He did not purpose the wilderness to destroy us, but to *empower* us, and we must individually commit ourselves to completing this journey. Our pursuit towards God in the wilderness is vital for us to be healed from our past, live freely in our present and become equipped for our future. Are we willing to be alone with God? God desires to sup with all of us and He wants to use us for His Glory. He wants us to demonstrate our faith by fulfilling our purpose, and we must begin in the wilderness.

Years before I ever was given this book to write, God gave me a dream and its spiritual interpretation:

> My family and I were in our car, driving on the highway, traveling home. **Home is our place of rest; God's presence.** Suddenly the highway was jam packed with traffic. **We all seek to get to God's presence.** Every lane was crowded and we were wedged in the middle of it. **We are often stuck in mediocrity and normality with everyone else.** I saw

Preface

an opening to get off the highway so we got off, desperately seeking an alternative route home. **We seek God's presence, but usually in our own abilities.** As I began searching for an easier way to get my family and I home, it became evident that all other roads were closed and my only option was to get back on the highway. **There is only one way to the Presence of God.** So, we got back on the highway. **The Highway is our wilderness.** We went through a cycle of getting off the highway to find a different route home, to then being forced back onto the highway. **We all experience our stages of stubbornness.** I finally surrendered to the fact that it was hopeless to find another way home. **We must choose to submit to God's way – through the wilderness.** We began to maneuver through the traffic on the highway to get further along. **We try to hasten our way to God.** All the while, I was aggravated and perplexed about the huge delay that we were experiencing. **Though we submit to His way, we don't always understand the trials and delays of the wilderness.** As we created a path through the traffic (**we can't stand being stuck in one place**), I observed that other cars were following us and were relying on us to get them through the traffic jam as well. **We are a constant example to others and they depend on us to lead them out of their obstacle.** What was so peculiar was the fact that the highway was enormous and there were plenty of lanes to allow the traffic to keep moving, even with a couple of accidents on the road. **We all have the opportunity to access God without interference.** However, when we wander and are lost, we cause delays for ourselves and others that are around us.** While our patience began to run thin (**we get tired and frustrated of the delays to reach God**), I saw giant anchors coming out of the sea by the highway. **We have saints and religious leaders who give up on God and turn away from Him.** The anchors were massive (**these are highly influential religious leaders**) and they were landing right onto the highway (**these influences block us from the Presence of God**). There were so many anchors landing on the road (**so many saints turn from God to their own way**) that we felt that if we stopped moving we would never make it home. **We are often so influenced by these leaders and their teachings, that they literally prevent us from being in the Presence of God.** As I took my eyes off the sea and the anchors, I desperately began to focus on the road. **We must stop depending on leaders and their teachings – just because of who they are – and focus on our own personal wilderness experience.** I passed by cars that were trapped because an anchor landed on or in front of their car. **Rather than God, we become fascinated by the religious leaders' teachings.** I even noticed that some of the cars that were following me were also left behind because an anchor blocked their way. **We depend on the lives of others for direction – instead of God – so, when someone tells us what we want to hear, we are prohibited from moving forward.** Everyone else was so focused on the anchors that they forgot to keep moving and became stuck in their lanes. **We become distracted from our purpose**

Preface

in God, focus on the teachings of men and become trapped. As we reached the front of the traffic we began to rejoice, and after a long winding journey we finally had made it home! **When we endure the journey through the wilderness, we realize that we are free and have gained the knowledge of His purpose for us and the liberty to live in God's presence.**

God is waiting for our response to His Call. Will we remain stuck in traffic or will we disregard our own ways and enter into the Presence of God?

> **"The voice of him that crieth in the wilderness, Prepare ye the way of the LORD, make straight in the desert a highway for our God. (Isaiah 40:3)**

Introduction

"And Jesus, when he was baptized, went up straightway out of the water: and, lo, the heavens were opened unto him, and he saw the Spirit of God descending like a dove, and lighting upon him: And lo a voice from heaven, saying, This is my beloved Son, in whom I am well pleased. Then was Jesus led up of the Spirit into the wilderness to be tempted of the devil. And when he had fasted forty days and forty nights, he was afterward an hungred." (Matthew 3:16, 4:2)

What is so important about the wilderness? Why does it take such a dry and lonely place for us to grow in God? Why did *Jesus* have to go to the wilderness?

The first place that Jesus went after being baptized by John the Baptist was the wilderness. He had just been proclaimed to be the Son of God by the Father. Everyone at the Jordan River heard John the Baptist's proclamation of who Jesus was. So what is so special about the wilderness that even Jesus was led there? Jesus, like others in the bible, had a wilderness experience in preparation for His ministry. Just imagine not eating for *four* days, not to mention *forty*! Jesus was nourishing his inner (*spirit*) man, while his *flesh* was being deprived of its nourishment. It wasn't the fact that He was not hungry, but he sacrificed his natural desires to quench His spiritual desire - to be empowered by the Spirit. In His

Introduction

solitude, Jesus ate of wisdom, understanding, knowledge – He ate of the Spirit of God. Jesus' flesh had to come in alignment with His spirit so that He could fulfill His destiny as the Lamb of God. *Could you see Jesus accepting Satan's offers?* Jesus was tempted in every way but his flesh was never allowed to make decisions.

> "For we have not an high priest which cannot be touched with the feeling of our infirmities; but was in all points tempted like as we are, yet without sin." (Hebrews 4:15)

The wilderness placed Jesus in an extreme natural condition to produce an extreme dependence on the Spirit of God. Jesus could do nothing unless the Father told Him. Jesus' oneness with the Father's will and plan was attributed to His time alone in the Presence of God. God desires to have the same oneness that He had with Jesus Christ, with *us*. (John 17:21-22)

God does not want us fearful and confused about His purpose for our lives. God wants to become one with us so we can fulfill what He's purposed for us to do from the time of our creation. Our oneness with God will equip us with the same power that Jesus had in His earthly ministry. However, we must humbly submit to change so that we can be one with God.

> "If a man therefore purge himself from these, he shall be a vessel unto honour, sanctified, and meet for the master's use, and prepared unto every good work." (2 Timothy 2:21)

Encampment # 1

THE WILDERNESS OF SHUR

"So Moses brought Israel from the Red sea, and they went out into the wilderness of Shur; and they went three days in the wilderness, and found no water."

Exodus 15:22

The Wilderness

"Until the spirit be poured upon us from on high, and the wilderness be a fruitful field, and the fruitful field be counted for a forest. Then judgment shall dwell in the wilderness, and righteousness remain in the fruitful field." (Isaiah 32:15-16)

The wilderness is a place where there is no water; it is a dry and desperate place. It is a place that produces no increase and drives us into exhaustion. The wilderness is a place where faith is tried and where every weakness is exposed. It has no shade from the sun and no escape from the heat. The wilderness is a place that every believer has to experience to be molded for their divine purpose.

Jesus is such a loving God; He understands the necessity for us to experience the wilderness. He knows that the wilderness will mold, nurture, and prepare us for our calling. We have to appreciate the time God invests in us, and embrace His divine ways to refine us.

Naturally the wilderness is not a place that *we* would choose to go. Most of us would say the wilderness is not necessary to grow stronger with the Lord.

"And he said unto him, Lord, I am ready to go with thee, both into prison, and to death. And he said, I tell thee, Peter, the cock shall not crow this day, before that thou shalt thrice deny that thou knowest me." (Luke 22:33-34)

As Peter we feel we are ready to walk in our purpose but when it is all said and done we deny Jesus just like Peter did. This is one reason so many of us never grow in our faith because we are uncomfortable with change. We say that our journey in life needs not validation; but the wilderness does just that – it validates our testimony. We will gladly accept the blessings of God but will bail out when it requires submitting to Him. We want the benefits of a relationship with God but refuse to commit completely to Him. Jesus was preparing Peter for his wilderness experience but Peter could not understand that the sifting process was necessary for him to be submitted to the divine purpose and plan for his life.

> "And the Lord said, Simon, Simon, behold, Satan hath desired to have you, that he may sift you as wheat: But I have prayed for thee, that thy faith fail not: and when thou art converted, strengthen thy brethren." (Luke 22:31-32)

Jesus has prayed over us that our faith in Him will not fail but rather be strengthened by the process we go through. Peter had to be humbled so that he had no confidence in his abilities but was dependant on God for strength. We can be confident that no matter what we go through in the wilderness God has already prayed for us.

In the wilderness we will not only be given the wisdom and direction of how God wants to use our talents and gifts, but it will also get "self" out of the equation. Every avenue and resource we have dries up and becomes useless in the wilderness. We are not able to do anything in ourselves that will become successful because nothing can grow in a dry desert place. God withdraws everything from us to preserve us and instruct us spiritually.

OUR JOURNEY BEGINS

God reveals to us our divine purpose and He feeds us His word through revelations, dreams, the bible, and prayer. Every word that God gives to us has to be tried to be effective for His use. Before the wilderness we have just experienced our initial revelation of our divine purpose through the calling of God. He needs us to see that our purpose can only be accomplished in Him and *His* power – not through *our* power. The wilderness is our pathway to a victorious life in God. He does not send us another way because He does not want us to fail or give up.

> "And it came to pass, when Pharaoh had let the people go, that God led them not through the way of the land of the Philistines, although that was near; for God said, Lest peradventure the people repent when they see war, and they return to Egypt: But God led the people about, through the way of the wilderness of the Red sea: and the children of Israel went up harnessed out of the land of Egypt." (Exodus 13:17-18)

Although God desires to try our hearts, purify us and strengthen us, we will not *voluntarily* choose to go through the wilderness. The wilderness is the "road less traveled." It is the route that *seems* to lead to death, but it is actually the way that leads to life and genuine power! This special, life changing experience convinces us that God is real and then we decide to live for Him completely. This is where our journey begins!

Encampment # 2

MARAH

"And when they came to Marah, they could not drink of the waters of Marah, for they were bitter: therefore the name of it was called Marah."

Exodus 15:23

Supply in Drought

"And Jesus answered him, saying, It is written, That man shall not live by bread alone, but by every word of God." (Luke 4:4)

In our lives, we are accustomed to always depending on people (our parents, family and friends). When we run into trouble, we never appreciate or depend on God to satisfy our needs. We know how to manipulate people and get them to give us the things we need or want. It is easy to manipulate people that love us and are concerned for us because they don't want to see us suffer. So, we always look for them when we can't pay a bill, when we need food, or are just in need for *something*. These individuals that help us don't realize that by them always coming to our rescue, they are hindering us from spiritual growth, and seeing that it is God who will supply our needs.

We can say we believe God can supply our needs, but we try to avoid going through the experiences where He is trying to prove it to us. Experiences such as having no money and our bank accounts are depleted, a broken down car, or we need groceries but barely have enough just to pay the rent. Our friends and family are not available to aid us, and all we can do is cry to God for help. As we pray, we give God our problems

Supply in Drought

and we receive peace in spite of our situation. Next thing we know, someone calls and says they want to take us grocery shopping and we can get whatever we want! We did not ask or manipulate anyone, but *God* used them to supply our need.

This revelation allows God to unveil Himself to us as The Supplier. We store our possessions in fear of what might happen in the future, while God supplies – through His love – to meet every need according to our situation. God does not want us to lean on our *own* supply to finance *His* vision. What He has in store is far greater than what our resources can handle, so He breaks us down and He strips off the limitations that we have placed on our purpose.

When we involve *our* resources, we limit God's supply to overflow and exceed our natural expectations. When we fall into trouble we lean on our own resources to get out, which prevents opportunities for miracles to occur in our life. If we use only what we see, we can't tap into the unseen resources that God has placed in front of our situations. Will we trust God to supply and satisfy the needs of His people or will we reject the opportunity for Him to work a miracle through us? God wants to empty our hands so that He can fill them with purpose and power. We can never fulfill God's purpose when we are still holding onto "things" that are from our past.

THE POWER OF EMPTY HANDS

Many times my two oldest boys help me with chores around the house. When I call them to help me, they come to me with their hands full of toys. I tell them to empty their hands so they can effectively accomplish what I need them to do. Sometimes they forget to empty their hands and they

Humbly Submitting to Change

struggle to fulfill my request. They exert more energy than what is necessary to complete the job that I feel is easy. When their hands are empty, they can see a difference, and they don't feel burdened down with hard work. They finish my request quickly and come back eagerly looking for more work to do.

God regards *us* in the same way. He does not give us hard and complicated assignments to do, but He gives us assignments according to the gifts and talents He has placed inside of us.

Like my boys and I, when God calls us, we come to Him with our hands full (with pleasures, clutter, failures, insecurities, doubts, lusts, pride, scars, secrets, and much more). He assigns us a task but it takes forever for us to complete it because we refuse to let go of *our* "toys". We work so hard to accomplish a simple task that by the time we are done we want to take a break and rest, before we see if there is another assignment. We struggle to do many mighty acts in God because we don't want to lose our "toys". We are so focused on ourselves and what we have, that we try to complete our assignments, while holding our "toys" in our hands to avoid anyone else from playing with them.

God sees that we are ineffective in completing our assignments, so He instructs us to trust Him and let go of the "toys" so that we can work more effectively. "And said unto them, Hear me, ye Levites, sanctify now yourselves, and sanctify the house of the LORD God of your fathers, and carry forth the filthiness out of the holy place." (II Chronicles 29:5) When we let go of the "toys" we begin to realize that our tasks are easier because God can now place His power in our empty hands. "And Hezekiah rejoiced, and all the people, that God had prepared the people: for the thing was done suddenly." (II Chronicles 29:36) We see the benefit of approaching Him empty handed and we become zealous stewards of the power that He has placed in our hands. We eagerly ask God for our next assignment and allow Him to supply us with the purpose and power required for it. We forget about our old "toys" as they are replaced with a new desire to successfully accomplish His work. The wilderness is the place where we are instructed to let go of our old "toys," then we receive our divine assignment and we become filled with genuine power and divine purpose.

SUPPLIED TO DELIVER

> "And the LORD looked upon him, and said, Go in this thy might, and thou shalt save Israel from the hand of the Midianites: have not I sent thee?" (Judges 6:14)

God told Gideon that he was going to deliver the people of Israel from out of the hands of their enemies. "And he said unto him, Oh my Lord, wherewith shall I save Israel? behold, my family is poor in Manasseh, and I am the least in my father's house." (Judges 6:15) Gideon did not see what God saw in him, but God spoke to the man Gideon was created to be, not the man he had been. "And the angel of the LORD appeared unto him, and said unto him, The LORD is with thee, thou mighty man of valour." (Judges 6:12) God used a man to impact his entire generation that in the world's eyes – was a "nobody". Gideon was not even regarded as important in his father's house. Just like Gideon, it is our divine destiny to do great things for the kingdom of God. No matter what the world thinks about us, only God's calling over our lives matters. When it came time for Israel's deliverance, God told Gideon:

Humbly Submitting to Change

"And the LORD said unto Gideon, The people that are with thee are too many for me to give the Midianites into their hands, lest Israel vaunt themselves against me, saying, Mine own hand hath saved me." (Judges 7:2)

There were too many people in Gideon's army for God to get the glory and not man. God did not want Israel to think that they had the ability to win the battle on their own. It is possible that Gideon had the thought "man we need all the help we can get to defeat the Midianites". Gideon had thirty two thousand people on his side, but only ten thousand really believed that God was going to deliver them, for they were not afraid.

Nevertheless God was not satisfied, the people were still too many. Will we trust God when the odds are not in our favor?

"So he brought down the people unto the water: and the LORD said unto Gideon, Every one that lappeth of the water with his tongue, as a dog lappeth, him shalt thou set by himself; likewise every one that boweth down upon his knees to drink. And the number of them that lapped, putting their hand to their mouth, were three hundred men: but all the rest of the people bowed down upon their knees to drink water. And the LORD said unto Gideon, By the three hundred men that lapped will I save you, and deliver the Midianites into thine hand: and let all the other people go every man unto his place." (Judges 7:5-7)

God chose three hundred men that were thirsty for deliverance. When you are genuinely thirsty, you are not worried about good manners or what others might think. God chose these men because they would not question the method of how God was going to deliver Israel, they would simply

Supply in Drought

obey Gideon's instructions. God did not supply Gideon with people concerned about their image, but rather people that were humble and peculiar – just like him. Are you one of the three hundred or are you blending in with majority? Will you step out of your comfort zone to do what is in your heart or will you be afraid to be different?

> "And he divided the three hundred men into three companies, and he put a trumpet in every man's hand, with empty pitchers, and lamps within the pitchers." (Judges 7:16)

Gideon and the three hundred were about to go up against the Midianites with trumpets, and pitchers with lamps inside of them. God gave Gideon, men that thought "outside of the box;" not one of the men asked for weapons or swords, but rather obeyed Gideon without hesitation.

God supplied Gideon and the men with everything they needed to free Israel from the hand of the Midianites. Gideon did not use his own strategic plans to defeat the Midianties but depended on God to exert His delivering power in midst of their extreme circumstance.

SUPPLIED WITH SUBSTANCE

Sometimes we can be unhappy with the supply that we receive. We are unsatisfied with what God gives, and look for the things we *don't* have instead of what we *do* have. However, the wilderness allows us to appreciate God's ability to supply any and everything that is needed to accomplish *His* plan for us. What He supplies is greater than anything carnal (money, visible objects); He supplies us with His power.

Humbly Submitting to Change

"And I say unto you, Ask, and it shall be given you; seek, and ye shall find; knock, and it shall be opened unto you. For every one that asketh receiveth; and he that seeketh findeth; and to him that knocketh it shall be opened. If a son shall ask bread of any of you that is a father, will he give him a stone? or if he ask a fish, will he for a fish give him a serpent? Or if he shall ask an egg, will he offer him a scorpion? If ye then, being evil, know how to give good gifts unto your children: how much more shall your heavenly Father give the Holy Spirit to them that ask him?" (Luke 11:9-13)

Are we asking for God to give us His Spirit? Or, are we busy asking for things? The Holy Spirit is the only power that can satisfy any need that is presented to us. His Spirit gives us an abundance of peace in situations that are naturally deemed impossible. Our purpose can only function properly if our source of power is the Holy Spirit. The Holy Spirit brings God's presence into our lives and translates into an outpouring of miracles in our atmosphere. God's power effectively consumes us and flows through us to meet our needs as well as and the needs of those around us.

In our obedience to God, He equips us with new resources and tools that draw us closer to His plan for our lives. When we begin to tap into God's supply we can become prosperous in our lives. We will also become unchanged by our situations for our trust is not in ourselves, but in the *true* supplier of our lives.

God's supply begins and ends with His Word. His Word creates the avenues of change, and it is by His Word that we reach fulfillment in our assignments. The Word of God is our weapon that God empowers us with in our trying times. It is what satisfies our spiritual hunger and thirst for the Presence of God. When we seek to find God in His Word we are empowered to fulfill His will for our lives.

Encampment # 3

ELIM

"And they came to Elim, where were twelve wells of water, and threescore and ten palm trees: and they encamped there by the waters."

Exodus 15:27

Comfort in a Dry Place

"… our flesh had no rest, but we were troubled on every side; without were fightings, within were fears. Nevertheless God, that comforteth those that are cast down…"
(2 Corinthians 7:5-6)

It is very difficult to be in a place where we are vulnerable and powerless. The wilderness is a place where all of our "avenues" of comfort are closed and our hope is in the hands of an invisible God. Everything seems to be going wrong and our lives are being flipped upside down. The people that depend on us for strength look to us for guidance as trouble surrounds them.

God is truly trying our hearts during this desperate time. He is our comforter but He is looking for a resting place in us. It is a place where His comfort can effectively change us in the midst of our troubles. God wants to strengthen us through our trials. If we don't allow God to comfort us in our overwhelming situations, we will remain weak and dependant on carnal things to deliver us from our situations. It is a humbling experience to know that we can't get ourselves out of a situation without the Comfort of God. To be comforted by God is a promise that few of us ever receive, because we are consumed with controlling our situations to avoid being vulnerable.

MOLDED TO OVERCOME

Out of our trials, we can become Survivors or Overcomers; the difference is in the testimony of the two. Many of us are satisfied with just surviving our trials and not having to open ourselves to God's comfort.

A Survivor depends on the support and love of people in their time of need. An Overcomer receives strength from God, allowing Him to have full control and results in walking victoriously out of their problem. A Survivor has evidence of their trial (scars, debt, medication, etc.); an Overcomer is freed from the problem completely with no signs they were ever in the midst of the storm.

Survivors remain weak after the storm has past. In a situation where someone has survived deadly disease, they still have ailments caused by the disease. They continue to take medication to "prevent" a relapse, and are burdened with huge medical bills to pay. This individual may have survived their battle with the disease but will have to live their life with wounds from the battle.

On the other hand, an Overcomer is *strengthened* in the storm and receives the weapons of God to fight the spiritual battle. They are shielded against the attacks of the devil through faith, prayer, and the Word of God. "And he that overcometh, and keepeth my works unto the end, to him will I give power over the nations."(Revelations 2:26) They allow God to work a miracle in their life by "getting out of the way." When God is done with them, there is no work that is left undone. He heals them completely, He satisfies all their debt, and gives them *His* medication (The Word of God) to keep them healthy. This overcomer can then tell their testimony and allow someone else to be delivered from a situation.

The wilderness experience transforms us from Survivors to Overcomers. "He that overcometh shall inherit all things; and I will be his God, and he shall be my son." (Revelations 21:7) The things that try to oppress us have no power compared to the power of God. He created everything, *even* our situation and He is the only remedy for the problem.

THE COMFORT OF PRAYER

God's comfort is effectively "mixed" through our prayers. A prayer by a humble and contrite spirit can grab the attention of God and it begins the stirring process that brings out the gift that is within. Prayer takes our faith and aligns it with the Word of God. Prayer suppresses our fleshly desires that hinder us from growth in God and illuminates the gifts that God has placed in each of us.

The wilderness provokes passionate prayers because it becomes the only place we can find comfort. In the wilderness God literally shakes us and knocks our life off balance which makes us insecure and uncomfortable in ourselves and in others. When we can't find comfort in the things of the world, He grabs our attention and draws us to heartfelt communication with Him. Our prayers change from "I want *this* Lord," and "Do *that* for me, Lord," to "Father, I need your Presence," or "I want to be pleasing in Your sight," and "Take my life and use it your way."

Comfort in a Dry Place

Nehemiah prayed a passionate prayer when he heard about the affliction in Jerusalem. He was moved with compassion for God's people and wept and prayed before God. Nehemiah understood that *only* God could change the affliction in the holy city of Jerusalem.

During Nehemiah's time in prayer and fasting, God spoke purpose into his heart. He received his assignment from God, but had to wait upon Him to open the door for him to walk into his assignment. Through prayer, God comforted Nehemiah to not take matters into his own hands but to wait for *Him* to make a way. Resting in God's comfort, Nehemiah was prepared for his divine purpose, and equipped with the resources needed to rebuild Jerusalem's walls.

Before journeying to Jerusalem, Nehemiah's prayers comforted his heart to know that God was with him. So, when adversaries came, Nehemiah was not afraid, for God was with him. Nehemiah was faced with constant adversity while working to complete the restoration of Jerusalem's wall. Each time, however, God comforted and encouraged Nehemiah to stay focused on the task at hand. God's comfort also places *us* at ease when our enemies attempt to prevent His work. When our focus is on God, He can instruct us of His true purpose for us. How comforting it is to be in the plan of God that will ultimately impact *generations*!

When we begin to unlock our heart and mind to God, it allows Him to show us a deeper level of His comfort. Whatever comes our way, we are subject to *His* power and not our own. His presence is true comfort in knowing that we can't be defeated in Him. We can be bold and confident in facing our adversity because our Father is going to take care of us. When we enter into God's presence we become consumed with true Comfort because we know that *wherever* He takes us, He will also *keep* us.

Encampment # 4

WILDERNESS OF SIN

"And they took their journey from Elim, and all the congregation of the children of Israel came unto the wilderness of Sin, which is between Elim and Sinai, on the fifteenth day of the second month after their departing out of the land of Egypt."
Exodus 16:1

Built to Last

"Yea, forty years didst thou sustain them in the wilderness, so that they lacked nothing; their clothes waxed not old, and their feet swelled not." (Nehemiah 9:21)

In our society we are trained to become self sustaining; to sustain ourselves and take care of ourselves is perceived as being successful. This is a place carnally that men strive to get to. We take pride in being able to support our family's needs and wants. To start our adult lives physically, with very little (finances, property, assets, etc.), and then reach a level of success, we want to feel that we accomplished things all on our own.

We selfishly pursue money and glory to validate our lives. We allow society to determine our net worth by how much money we make and we limit our spiritual worth in God. We build our financial portfolios, we create resumes, and we get college degrees and distinctions. These things give us a sense of accomplishment and our reputations are considered honorable and noteworthy. All these accomplishments are evidence to everyone that we are successful people that are doing great things in our lives.

This mindset has poisoned the church, we have become so self-promoting that we have no time to promote *Jesus*. We are eager to gain titles and positions so that others will look at us with high regard. We want the benefits of having the titles of Apostle, Bishop, Prophet or Pastor without fulfilling the work of *that* title. All of the titles, all of the money, all of the degrees and all of the jobs are of no use in the wilderness. Not one thing that we carry into the wilderness will be able to sustain us through it.

SUSTAINED BY A DREAM

"And Joseph dreamed a dream, and he told it his brethren: and they hated him yet the more. And he said unto them, Hear, I pray you, this dream which I have dreamed: For, behold, we were binding sheaves in the field, and, lo, my sheaf arose, and also stood upright; and, behold, your sheaves stood round about, and made obeisance to my sheaf. And his brethren said to him, Shalt thou indeed reign over us? or shalt thou indeed have dominion over us? And they hated him yet the more for his dreams, and for his words. (Genesis 37:5-8)

Joseph – like many of *us* before being placed in the wilderness – was spoiled, arrogant and proud. He was highly favored by his father more than his brothers were, and in being treated *differently*, was not given many of the responsibilities that his brothers had. Joseph *enjoyed* being treated differently than his brothers and when God blessed him with dreams, he *could not* wait to tell them all about it. In Joseph's immaturity he failed to realize that he had no interpretation of these great dreams.

We sometimes feel that *we* are special when God reveals things to us and we are eager to share it with others.

Humbly Submitting to Change

However, without understanding, we will only cause confusion and strife. God knows that when we receive powerful revelations like Joseph, He must humble us first so the revelation can be manifested in our lives. In the midst of arrogance and boastfulness, God has mercy upon us and plants His divine purpose in our lives. We envision that what God has placed in our hearts, we will experience without struggle. Yet, God's path for Joseph was different than what Joseph anticipated, just how it will be different for us. We must be humiliated before we see the fulfillment of God's divine plan for our lives. "By humility and the fear of the LORD are riches, and honour, and life." (Proverbs 22:4)

All of Joseph's brothers wanted to kill him out their hatred for him and his dreams, *except* for his oldest brother, Reuben. Reuben did not want to kill his little brother though he just wanted to teach young Joseph a lesson.

> "Come now therefore, and let us slay him, and cast him into some pit, and we will say, Some evil beast hath devoured him: and we shall see what will become of his dreams. And Reuben heard it, and he delivered him out of their hands; and said let us not kill him. And Reuben said unto them, Shed no blood, but cast him into this pit that is in the wilderness, and lay no hand upon him; that he might rid him out of their hands, to deliver him to his father again. And it came to pass, when Joseph was come unto his brethren, that they stripped Joseph out of his coat, his coat of many colours that was on him; And they took him, and cast him into a pit: and the pit was empty, there was no water in it." (Genesis 37:22-24)

Teaching Joseph a lesson, they strip him of his proud clothes and threw him into the pit of the wilderness. Has anyone ever thrown you into a pit in efforts to teach you a lesson? Reuben thought he was just appeasing his brothers' desire to punish Joseph, but in their ignorance they were actually fulfilling the will of God. In the pit where Joseph was stripped of his beautiful garments, he was left in a place where there was no life or water. He was humiliated. Yes, Reuben and his brothers accomplished their goal of teaching Joseph a lesson, but God was not through with Joseph just yet. "And Reuben returned unto the pit; and, behold, Joseph was not in the pit; and he rent his clothes." (Genesis 37:29)

SUBMITTING TO PROSPERITY

Joseph was sold into slavery by his brothers for money and taken to Egypt. He was taken from all that he knew, and had to find comfort in being a slave in Egypt. This is where most of us throw in the towel and quit on God. Is it God's will for me to be a slave? How could God let such a thing happen to me, his chosen servant? Being a slave, Joseph did not express these emotions, as most of us would, he just submitted himself to God and God allowed him to prosper in his circumstance.

> "And the LORD was with Joseph, and he was a prosperous man; and he was in the house of his master the Egyptian. And his master saw that the LORD was with him, and that the LORD made all that he did to prosper in his hand. And Joseph found grace in his sight, and he served him: and he made him overseer over his house, and all that he had he put into his hand." (Genesis 39:2-4)

Through Joseph's submission, his master saw that the Lord was with Joseph. He also saw that it was not Joseph's gifts or wisdom that made him special; it was just his relationship with God that made him to prosper. When we are obedient to those that have rule over us, God is able to be seen and *His* Presence allows us to prosper even in our low positions. Though Joseph had found favor in the sight of his master, this was not Joseph's resting place.

LIBERATED IN BONDAGE

Joseph had prospered greatly as a slave, but after his master's wife lied on him, he found himself bound in prison. Although he was a prisoner, he was not forsaken by God; it was his destiny to be in that prison. The entire time God was with Joseph, as He is with us no matter what has us bound, and His mercy is ever-present.

> "But the LORD was with Joseph, and shewed him mercy, and gave him favour in the sight of the keeper of the prison. And the keeper of the prison committed to Joseph's hand all the prisoners that were in the prison; and whatsoever they did there, he was the doer of it." (Genesis 39:21-22)

Joseph was a prisoner, yet he was *free* while in prison. He was not like the other prisoners, for he was given rule over them. It was not because Joseph had great leadership qualities, but rather God was with him. When we are aware that God is with us wherever our paths take us, we are liberated from the bondage of our circumstances.

In Joseph's liberation, God was able to equip him with the gift of interpretation. "And they said unto him, We have dreamed a dream, and there is no interpreter of it. And Joseph said unto them, Do not interpretations belong to God? tell me them, I pray you." (Genesis 40:8) Joseph was blessed to have divine dreams, but now he could understand the meanings of those dreams because he rested his hope in *God*, not *himself.*

When Joseph interpreted the dream of the butler, he tried to use his gift to get himself out of prison. He hadn't yet understood that *God* placed him in prison, so he blamed other people for him being in the midst of the dungeon.

> "But think on me when it shall be well with thee, and shew kindness, I pray thee, unto me, and make mention of me unto Pharaoh, and bring me out of this house: For indeed I was stolen away out of the land of the Hebrews: and here also have I done nothing that they should put me into the dungeon." (Genesis 40:14-15)

We place the blame of our circumstances on others, not comprehending that God has placed us there for the sole purpose of *using* us. When we see a way out of our situation we look for man to deliver us out of bondage, instead of the one that has *sustained* us in bondage. When we depend on man they will always disappoint us. "Yet did not the chief butler remember Joseph, but forgat him." (Genesis 40:23) Joseph stayed in prison two more years after he had interpreted the dream for the butler, but God sustained Joseph for such a time like this.

> "Then Pharaoh sent and called Joseph, and they brought him hastily out of the dungeon: and he shaved himself, and changed his raiment, and came in unto Pharaoh. And Pharaoh said unto Joseph, I have dreamed a dream, and there is none that can interpret it: and I have heard say of thee, that thou canst understand a dream to interpret it. And Joseph answered Pharaoh, saying, It is not in me: God shall give Pharaoh an answer of peace." (Genesis 41:14-16)

DIVINELY PLACED

Joseph had been divinely placed to perform the Will of God in the midst of an ungodly kingdom. Suddenly he was taken from prison, shaved and given new clothes before even entering the presence of the Pharaoh. God kept Joseph through rejection, the pit, slavery *and* prison, all for the purpose of conditioning him to perform His will and keep God's promise to Abraham alive.

> "And Pharaoh said unto his servants, Can we find such a one as this is, a man in whom the Spirit of God is? And Pharaoh said unto Joseph, Forasmuch as God hath shewed thee all this, there is none so discreet and wise as thou art: Thou shalt be over my house, and according unto thy word shall all my people be ruled: only in the throne will I be greater than thou. And Pharaoh said unto Joseph, See, I have set thee over all the land of Egypt." (Genesis 41:38-41)

Joseph had been humbled, and through God's mercy he was then promoted to his ordained position. God had orchestrated Joseph's path even *before* Joseph was born. When God promised Abraham, Isaac, and Jacob that Israel would be a great nation, it was through Joseph's life that He fulfilled the promise of a nation coming from the seed of Abraham. If Joseph had not gone to Egypt, Jacob and his family would have died from starvation. Nevertheless, through the affliction of *one*, God preserved many. As with Joseph, through the affliction that *we* persevere, many will be saved.

It is necessary for us to submit ourselves to God so that He can perform His Purpose through us. During Joseph's affliction, God blessed him and made him prosperous *in spite of* his affliction. "And Joseph called the name of the firstborn Manasseh: For God, said he, hath made me forget all my toil, and all my father's house. And the name of the second called he Ephraim: For God hath caused me to be fruitful in the land of my affliction." (Genesis 41:51-52)

PURPOSE OF AFFLICTION

In his new position, Joseph could *then* see why God had taken him through the path of affliction and he no longer blamed anyone for causing him to suffer; rather, he understood it was God's will.

> "Now therefore be not grieved, nor angry with yourselves, that ye sold me hither: for God did send me before you to preserve life. For these two years hath the famine been in the land: and yet there are five years, in the which there shall neither be earing nor harvest. And God sent me before you to preserve you a posterity in the earth, and to save your lives by a great deliverance." (Genesis 45:5-7)

It may have been thirteen *long* years of affliction for Joseph, but it was worth it all because his family was saved. In the end, Joseph understood that in the fulfillment of his dream, it was not *him* that was great but *God*.

God keeps us by confirming that what He has planned for us is greater than what we are going through. He wants to show us that no matter what we might go through – though it might seem hopeless and barren – He is able to sustain us through the famine. "Cast thy burden upon the LORD, and he shall sustain thee: he shall never suffer the righteous to be moved." (Psalms 55:22) God is able to keep us and preserve us so that we are able to be molded into what He has created us to be. If we just hold onto His promise He will make good what He has established in our hearts.

Encampment # 5

REPHIDIM

"And all the congregation of the children of Israel journeyed from the wilderness of Sin, after their journeys, according to the commandment of the LORD, and pitched in Rephidim: and there was no water for the people to drink."
Exodus 17:1

Alone with God

"Seemeth it but a small thing unto you, that the God of Israel hath separated you from the congregation of Israel, to bring you near to himself to do the service of the tabernacle of the LORD, and to stand before the congregation to minister unto them?" (Numbers 16:9)

    I am naturally a social person. I can make friends easily and can relate usually to anyone, so, for me to be placed in the wilderness was bewildering because it made me vulnerable. I wanted to share with everyone the purpose that God had placed in me. However, when I would speak the words God gave me, my friends, family and church family would not receive it. My words were ineffective, and every time, I would regret that I said anything at all. Deep down I was looking for validation from others, that what I was saying and doing was the "right thing." How frustrating it was to speak God's words and no one be impacted by the message! The problem was that I was seeking *man's* validation while God was teaching me that *His* approval was all that mattered.

    When the messages we have are not received by others, we begin to seclude ourselves from them, not recognizing that we are in the wilderness. We become lonely, discontent with everyone, and as we distance ourselves we begin to lose touch with our friends, family, and church family.

RECONNECTED TO GOD

Throughout our lives we have a number of relationships that we build. We are *born* into our first relationships – our families – that initially mold us and shape us. We usually draw close to the family members that have similar tastes and personalities. Drawn by our desires and feelings, we enjoy the presence of the people that we have a strong connection with. We have a sense of comfort and security when we are around them, and we tend to let our guard down. In our loving relationships, we learn what love is as well as how to receive and give love. As we grow, we build bonds with other people from our schools, churches and other surroundings. Our friends and family become at ease with us and appreciate who we are; they enjoy our presence and take pride in having us in their lives. Nevertheless, as time moves on, so does many of our relationships. The connections we once had come to an end as we change schools, churches, go to colleges, or even change locations. We then form new relationships with new people and we begin to assimilate to our new environment.

Our families hold on to the memories of our childhood, as they try to stay connected to us. For our entire lives, we have been defined by the people we were connected to. They gave us nicknames, told us what we were good at, told us what the standard of success was, and they were our examples of marriage. Our bonds and relationships impact every one of the choices we make – the right relationships help us make the right choices, while the wrong relationships lead us to bad choices. This is the reason why our wilderness journey is so important; it takes the connections we have to our friends and loved ones and disconnects us, in order for us to be reconnected to God. "Therefore if any man be in Christ, he is a new creature: old things are passed away; behold, all things are become new." (II Corinthians 5:17) We will never see or hear from God as long as we try to hold on to the very relationships that God has disconnected us from. When maintained, these relationships choke our purpose and destroy our connection to hearing from God. "And that which fell among thorns are they, which, when they have heard, go forth, and are choked with cares and riches and pleasures of this life, and bring no fruit to perfection." (Luke 8:14)

Many times when we hear a word from God, we try to apply it to our lives without receiving complete understanding first. We separate ourselves and distance ourselves from people because we feel we are on "another level" and that we can't "dirty" ourselves with who we feel are *unfruitful* people. The wilderness takes this pride and high-mindedness that we have and shows us that *we* are the ones that need to be cleansed; *we* are the sinners, *we* are the unproductive people and *we* are in need of a true relationship with God. "Draw nigh to God, and he will draw nigh to you. Cleanse your hands, ye sinners; and purify your hearts, ye double minded." (James 4:8) We are disconnected from people because *we* are corrupt and are in need of God to instruct us on what He requires in every relationship that we have. "Yet hast thou not walked after their ways, nor done after their abominations: but, as if that were a very little thing, thou wast corrupted more than they in all thy ways." (Ezekiel 16:47)

TURNING FROM OUR "ELIAB"

For others, unfortunately, it is bewildering and upsetting to see *us* changing while *they* are not. They devalue our growth in God, and try to "chip away" at our spiritual armor. Their goal is to see us revert back to our old self and our old ways, so they can justify that ultimately, we have *not* changed.

> "And Eliab his eldest brother heard when he spake unto the men; and Eliab's anger was kindled against David, and he said, Why camest thou down hither? and with whom hast thou left those few sheep in the wilderness? I know thy pride, and the naughtiness of thine heart; for thou art come down that thou mightest see the battle. And David said, What have I now done? Is there not a cause? And he turned from him toward another, and spake after the same manner: and the people answered him again after the former manner."
> (I Kings 17:28-30)

In this relationship between brothers, Eliab did not see the greatness in David. He just saw his little brother; in his ignorance he devalued the future King of Israel. Eliab actually witnessed David being anointed by Samuel to be King (I Samuel 16:13), but he wanted to keep David in the position He had always known him to be in. Eliab was blinded to David's relationship with God, and for that reason, he confused David's confidence in God for youthful pride. Through David's response, we see that Eliab most likely made a habit of accusing David of being mischievous and having a naughty heart. Nevertheless, David had no time to justify himself to his older brother; Eliab would never understand what God was about to do through David. David had to prepare himself for battle, so he turned away from his brother and turned towards

Humbly Submitting to Change

his destiny. Little did they know, Eliab and the rest of Israel were going to see God's delivering power through a "ruddy" young man that was after God's heart.

We must turn from *our* "Eliab" and set our faces toward *our* divine destiny. Our lives can not be consumed with trying to justify ourselves to others, but it must be in submission to our relationship with God. God had communed with David so much (in the wilderness while he was watching the sheep), that David had time to see the power of God. Eliab looked at David's job of watching the few sheep in the wilderness as something small and insignificant, but David was not alone he was with God.

Though others might place a reproach on the things we are doing, it is fortunately an opportunity for God to commune with us *alone*. He places us where our relationships *and* their influence have no power, which allows us to meet Our Father and learn to depend on Him solely. Our parents can't come to the rescue in the wilderness, and our friends can't give us their words of encouragement and support. We are alone with God as He unravels our past and shows us our destiny in Him. He shows us that our importance does not come from the relationships we have with *people*, but it comes from our relationship with *Him*.

THE DEADLY CONNECTION

There are certain people that are in our lives that have the ability to unarm us *spiritually*. They know how to say, do, and give the "right" things to manipulate us for their benefit. God is aware that if He does not separate us from these individuals, we will never walk in the power that He has ordained for our lives.

Our purpose is not for everyone it is for us. It is imperative that we guard it from others until God has fully developed us and we are molded for His use. Though we may be strong around everyone else, our *deadly connections* know exactly how to weaken us. They are not necessarily evil; but are not good for us. In the story of Samson we see he had a weakness for the opposite sex. He was strong, smart and skilled but, could not overcome his weakness for women that had no respect for His God.

> "And Samson went down to Timnath, and saw a woman in Timnath of the daughters of the Philistines. And he came up, and told his father and his mother, and said, I have seen a woman in Timnath of the daughters of the Philistines: now therefore get her for me to wife. Then his father and his mother said unto him, Is there never a woman among the daughters of thy brethren, or among all my people, that thou goest to take a wife of the uncircumcised Philistines? And Samson said unto his father, Get her for me; for she pleaseth me well." (Judges 14:1-3)

> "Then went Samson to Gaza, and saw there an harlot, and went in unto her. And it was told the Gazites, saying, Samson is come hither. And they compassed him in, and laid wait for him all night in the gate of the city, and were quiet all the night, saying, In the morning, when it is day, we shall kill him." (Judges 16:1-2)

> "And it came to pass afterward, that he loved a woman in the valley of Sorek, whose name was Delilah…" (Judges 16:4)

Humbly Submitting to Change

It must be noted that Samson did not have trouble with *every* woman, but the ones that he did were able to toil with his emotions in order to get what they wanted.

Our "Delilah" could be anyone. Just as Samson tried to guard his secrets and failed, so will we. We are vulnerable to these individuals and can't guard our purpose without the Help of God. We are emotionally entangled with them and we feel secure in their presence. We undress ourselves emotionally in front of them, which exposes us to attacks from the enemy. It is imperative that these deadly connections be destroyed before we leave the wilderness or the enemy will use them against us when we least expect it.

So many of us are like Samson – strong and gifted on the outside, while underneath we are weak and fragile. We never face the root of our weaknesses because we want to carry on our façade of being strong and highly skilled. We refuse to examine ourselves because deep down we are scared of who we *really* are. We have carried our masks for so long that if we stopped, we would not know how to survive. *What would people say? Everyone looks for me for strength, how can I come to grips with myself?*

Like Samson, we never realize that the problem is not the *person* with whom we have a relationship with, but the problem is *us*. We love being connected to *our* "Delilah"; *we* enjoy unarming ourselves around her. *We* are attracted to the woman in the valley "….that he loved a woman in the valley of Sorek, whose name was Delilah." (Judges 16:4) We know that these relationships are not beneficial to us, but we do not let go of them because we are captivated by their beauty. We never cut ties with these people because we don't want to feel the pain of being without them. These connections are the reason why so many of us wander through our lives and never obtain the promises of God. If we don't come to grips with our weaknesses and let go of ourselves *and* the relationships God has disconnected us from, we will stay stagnate and *never* reach our "Promise Land".

To much dismay, *our* "Delilah" does not have to *lie* to us to find out *our* secrets.

> "And Delilah said to Samson, Tell me, I pray thee, wherein thy great strength lieth, and wherewith thou mightest be bound to afflict thee." (Judges 16:6)

Some people are completely open about their agenda, but we feel we are strong enough to resist them. In Samson's case, we can see that Delilah's persistence weakened Samson and caused him to open up his heart to her. (Judges 16:15-18) When we open up to the wrong people we are placing ourselves in the chains of bondage. We cannot allow anyone to separate us from the Presence of God. Though we may be drawn by their beauty or influence, we have to resist the temptation to rest in the "lap of Delilah."

POWERFUL CONNECTIONS

As we begin to appreciate His presence and it becomes our habitation, we start to examine ourselves closely and value the treasures that God has given us. Life has changed and what we had envisioned for our lives has vanished with just a word from God. Now that we have a *real* relationship with God, He can bring purpose into the relationships that He will connect us to.

Humbly Submitting to Change

We will appreciate and love these people because there will be a purpose for the connection. There won't be a connection just because it is *family* or because they are *attractive.* We will be *divinely* connected, which will put God in the *center* of the relationships. "But now hath God set the members every one of them in the body, as it hath pleased him." (I Corinthians 12:18) We will be joined for a divine purpose to give God the glory. *God* wants to create our relationships so that we are able to fulfill His plan for our lives, *and* reach the Promised Land together. In our reliance on God to give us prosperous relationships, we are content with whomever God chooses to connect us to. We are not worried about superficial qualities in people but we are grateful for each person that God has placed in our lives.

> "David therefore departed thence, and escaped to the cave Adullam: and when his brethren and all his father's house heard it, they went down thither to him. And every one that was in distress, and every one that was in debt, and every one that was discontented, gathered themselves unto him; and he became a captain over them: and there were with him about four hundred men." (1 Samuel 22:1-2)

David was alone *and* hiding in a cave from Saul who was trying to kill him. God sent stressed, impoverished, and unhappy men to the cave to meet David. In David's exile from his country, God sends these rejected but very gifted men that related to the feelings of uncertainty that David was feeling.

David had nothing to offer them and they were not looking for anything from David except direction. What God was about to take David through, he could not go through alone, but he needed a company of warriors that would "have his back." David and the four hundred men built an undeniable connection, for they were cohesively dependant on God to change their situations. In their unification, they won many battles and were a vital part of David's ultimate reign as king. Know that it is not what we can do for each other, but rather what God can do through our unity. God connect us to people in our lowest moments so that He can be the drive of the relationship.

Encampment # 6

MOUNT HOREB

"Behold, I will stand before thee there upon the rock in Horeb; and thou shalt smite the rock, and there shall come water out of it, that the people may drink. And Moses did so in the sight of the elders of Israel."

Exodus 17:6

Following the Pillar

"And we know that all things work together for good to them that love God, to them who are the called according to his purpose." (Romans 8:28)

     As we hear His voice and commune with Him, God builds our *faith* in Him. How much *easier* it is to handle the pains of life, when we know that it is for our *good*. Thank God there is a *plan* for our suffering! We are counted worthy to be used by God. So, we should embrace God's way and continue to denounce our ways so that we can be led to the presence of God. "And the LORD went before them by day in a pillar of a cloud, to lead them the way; and by night in a pillar of fire, to give them light; to go by day and night: He took not away the pillar of the cloud by day, nor the pillar of fire by night, from before the people." (Exodus 13:21-22)

     Wherever the presence of God went, that is where the children of Israel journeyed. They did not have to go far to find Him, all they had to do was look up. God was with them as a pillar of a cloud, and as a pillar of fire (*the feet of their Deliverer*). (Revelations 10:1) Regardless if it was one day or two years, whenever the cloud rested or moved, Israel packed up all there belongings and faithfully journeyed to their next destination. If they took their focus off of the pillar that was covering the tabernacle, they would have been lost in the wilderness.

We do not have a *cloud* to look up to for direction, but we *do* have God's spirit *inside* of us, that desires to guide our lives in the way that we are to go. It is easy to follow the Spirit when we are comfortable with where He is taking us. Will we truly follow the Spirit when it seems like we are being led to certain disaster? Will we look at our circumstances as too great for us to overcome them? When the spies came back with a mixed report about their Promise Land, Israel reached a crossroads; ultimately, they refused to listen to *Caleb's* report. Israel, as a result, wandered in the wilderness for forty years. Will we trust God's guidance so that we can possess the land He has prepared for us? When we become fearful and insecure of God's direction we become lost in transition.

LOST IN TRANSITION

Many times we reach the brink of disaster because we are ignorant to our next step in God. We have seen glimpses of change occur in our lives and we have reached the summit of mountaintops that, before entering the wilderness, we could have *never* imagined climbing. God has not only prospered us to walk on the mountaintops of life, but he has also safely guided us through the valleys. God has empowered us to succeed in the things that He has purposed in our lives. After we have accomplished our divine assignments, *what do we do next?* We have indulged ourselves in our assignments so much, that we know them inside *and* out. We have taken dominion over our task and have left no stones unturned. We have seen God's power destroy our enemies and deliver us in

Humbly Submitting to Change

times of famine. The question, however, becomes redundant in our minds. *What do we do now?*

In this state of uncertainty, our lives have to be submitted back into the hands of our Maker. We have been molded to fulfill our divine assignment, but now we must surrender our defined structure to become clay again. We now must be molded again to climb to the top of our *next* mountaintop.

Yes, we have become skilled in our fields of expertise, but what we have learned can not help us to prosper in where God is about to take us. Many of us have grown so comfortable in ourselves that we are fearful to subject ourselves back to the feeling of uncertainty that the molding process brings. This crossroads is a dangerous place to be. If we decide reject God's guidance and stay in our comfortable positions, we will lose the surety of God's presence *and* His promises. We will never reach satisfaction with just our accomplishments without losing the closeness we have with our God. Regardless of how many battles we have gone through, there is always a greater assignment on the horizon. When we are satisfied with our success, in hindsight, we lose sight of God, and our lives are then defined by *us*, not *God*. We are then, in part, lost in transition; we are fearful of "losing it all," but are unaware that we have already lost the way to His presence.

We then begin to wander in a state of dryness, looking for the closeness that we thought we once had with God. We deceive ourselves, believing that God is still working on our behalf, and begin to carry out assignments that were not even given to us. In reality, our Teacher has moved on, but we are still stuck in our comfortable state. If we don't humble ourselves to the instructions of our God, we risk failing our course.

One of the greatest examples of being "lost in transition," is Elijah. "And Elijah the Tishbite, who was of the inhabitants of Gilead, said unto Ahab, As the Lord God of Israel liveth, before whom I stand, there shall not be dew nor rain these years, but according to my word." (I Kings 17:1) The prophet Elijah received a word from God to boldly speak a word to King Ahab. He then adhered to God's guidance and traveled to a brook where God commanded the ravens to bring Elijah bread. Elijah's next destination was to the house of the widow of Zarephath; there, God sustained him, the widow *and* the widow's son during the famine, until the fulfillment of his divine assignment. While waiting for instruction, Elijah witnessed the power of God revive the widow's son from death. It was, however, merely a stepping stone in comparison to what God was *about* to do through him.

In the fullness of time, God lead Elijah back into the presence of King Ahab and the children of Israel. God had prepared Elijah for the great and victorious demonstration at Mount Carmel. He was so confident in God's Word, that he mocked the evil prophets of Baal and challenged them to prove *their* god. Much to the king and the people's surprise, God sent fire from Heaven and the children of Israel humbled themselves before God and killed the prophets of Baal. Nonetheless, Elijah's assignment was not complete; the rain still had not come. It wasn't until he traveled to the top of Mount Carmel that Elijah saw the fulfilling of his divine assignment. (I Kings 18:42-44)

Humbly Submitting to Change

In spite of Elijah seeing the cloud approach the mountain, he did not have the opportunity to bask in the glory of witnessing the completion of God's assignment; the hand of the Lord led him down that mountain faster than King Ahab's chariot. (I Kings 18:45-46)

Elijah, led to the bottom of the mountain by the hand of God, felt uncertain of what was next.

> "Then Jezebel sent a messenger unto Elijah, saying, So let the gods do to me, and more also, if I make not thy life as the life of one of them by to morrow about this time. And when he saw that, he arose, and went for his life, and came to Beersheba, which belongeth to Judah, and left his servant there. But he himself went a day's journey into the wilderness, and came and sat down under a juniper tree: and he requested for himself that he might die; and said, It is enough; now, O LORD, take away my life; for I am not better than my fathers." (I Kings 19:2-4)

Elijah became fearful for his life when he heard that Jezebel wanted to kill him. He was unsure if God was going to let her, so he fled to the wilderness. He had done all that he was instructed to do and felt that, in his own eyes, his purpose was complete. He had been faithful to all that God gave him to do, but he was ignorant to what was next for him. Just like Elijah, *we* tell God that what we have done for Him is *enough*. We have labored hard and completed our course, *so why can't we just rest?* We have done all that He has asked us to do but our lives still seem to lead us to death.

> "And as he lay and slept under a juniper tree, behold, then an angel touched him, and said unto him, Arise and eat." (I Kings 19:5)

Following the Pillar

In our low point, God instructs us to arise and eat. When we have fallen unclear of where God is leading us, we must arise from feeling sorry for ourselves and eat of the Word of God. "And the angel of the LORD came again the second time, and touched him, and said, Arise and eat; because the journey is too great for thee." (I Kings 19:7) The journey is too great for us if we do not listen to the Spirit of God. We must arise from ourselves and eat God's Word or we will remain lost. The Word of God will sustain us until we are placed back into the presence of God.

> "And he arose, and did eat and drink, and went in the strength of that meat forty days and forty nights unto Horeb the mount of God. And he came thither unto a cave, and lodged there; and, behold, the word of the LORD came to him, and he said unto him, What doest thou here, Elijah?" (I Kings 19:8-9)

What doest thou here? God words are so precise. He is asking us, why are we lost? God has not *hid* His presence from us; actually, it is us who has lost our faith and trust in Him and have surrendered ourselves to our fears. *We* have left *His* presence. We want to complain about what others are doing to us and how our surrounding circumstances seem to be leading us astray, but like Elijah, we can not answer God's question.

> "And he said, I have been very jealous for the LORD God of hosts: for the children of Israel have forsaken thy covenant, thrown down thine altars, and slain thy prophets with the sword; and I, even I only, am left; and they seek my life, to take it away." (I Kings 19:10)

Why are we lost? God had not forsaken Elijah and He will not forsake us either. We must, however, surrender ourselves to *God* and not to our *assignments*.

Humbly Submitting to Change

"And he said, Go forth, and stand upon the mount before the LORD. And, behold, the LORD passed by, and a great and strong wind rent the mountains, and brake in pieces the rocks before the LORD; but the LORD was not in the wind: and after the wind an earthquake; but the LORD was not in the earthquake: And after the earthquake a fire; but the LORD was not in the fire: and after the fire a still small voice. And it was so, when Elijah heard it, that he wrapped his face in his mantle, and went out, and stood in the entering in of the cave. And, behold, there came a voice unto him, and said, What doest thou here, Elijah?" (I Kings 19:11-13)

If we ignore His still small voice and are fearful of the earthquake, the strong winds *and* the fire, we will miss out on the great move of God that He has prepared for us. Though Elijah only saw disarray, God was constructing greatness on behalf of His servant. God has no time to comfort our pity parties; He only wants to instruct us on what our next assignment will be. How *wonderful* it is to know that God has a great work for us to *still* accomplish!

"And the LORD said unto him, Go, return on thy way to the wilderness of Damascus: and when thou comest, anoint Hazael to be king over Syria:And Jehu the son of Nimshi shalt thou anoint to be king over Israel: and Elisha the son of Shaphat of Abelmeholah shalt thou anoint to be prophet in thy room. And it shall come to pass, that him that escapeth the sword of Hazael shall Jehu slay: and him that escapeth from the sword of Jehu shall Elisha slay. Yet I have left me seven thousand in Israel, all the knees which have not bowed unto Baal, and every mouth which hath not kissed him." (I Kings 19:15-18)

In Elijah's case, his next assignment led him to anoint kings, teach his successor, and reach his divine destination – Heaven. When we humbly submit ourselves to change, God has the ability to redefine us for *His* purpose. Although God's guidance may take us through many ups and downs, when we stay fastened to His presence and heed to His instructions, we will receive great enjoyment and excitement on the way to *our* divine destination.

Encampment # 7

DESERT OF SINAI

"For they were departed from Rephidim, and were come to the desert of Sinai, and had pitched in the wilderness; and there Israel camped before the mount."

Exodus 19:2

The Wisdom of God

"The fear of the LORD is the beginning of wisdom: and the knowledge of the holy is understanding." (Proverbs 9:10)

So many times we mistakenly feel that our actions are divinely instructed. We take on arrogance that whatever we touch or do will be successful and most importantly, we don't feel we need instructions from anyone. Unfortunately, we have become a generation that is consumed *and* completely in love with ourselves. We apply our focus and energy toward things that benefit us *first*. However, when we depend on our own knowledge and wisdom, we end in disaster. *Our* wisdom is limited to what we have experienced through life, school and family, and when controlled by past experiences we limit our future in God.

We cannot endure the wilderness with our own strength. We can't rely on our past experiences to get us through; rather, we must depend on the One that conquered the wilderness: Jesus Christ. As our lives are uncovered we see all the falsehood that we have allowed to define who we are. We are confused as to why we are going through our situation and every "wise choice" that we make falls short of bringing us out on top. Visually our world is flipped upside down and it seems that we will not overcome this situation.

The Wisdom of God

Why has the Spirit of God led us away from everything that we love to a place where there is no place to live but rather die? Will our hearts still worship a God that has seemingly left us to die?

Death is necessary for us to walk and dwell in the presence of God. The question is: *How bad do we want to be in His Presence?* The wilderness is what separates the real worshippers from the fakes. We all start the journey the same, but as the pressures of the wilderness begin to intensify, some of us give up hope and return back to the bondage of self-reliance that God has delivered us from. However, those of us that endure the pain and face the internal battle within, become recipients of what God values and earnestly wants to give to us: *His wisdom.*

"Trust in the LORD with all thine heart; and lean not unto thine own understanding. In all thy ways acknowledge him, and he shall direct thy paths. Be not wise in thine own eyes: fear the LORD, and depart from evil." (Proverbs 3:5-7) His wisdom is not just words of understanding; it is established through power from above. Now that we have accepted the presence of God in our lives and can grab hold of the intangible understanding of things visible and invisible, His word can be a lamp unto our feet because we rely on Him to feed us instructions. "Thy word is a lamp unto my feet, and a light unto my path." (Psalms 119:105)

We are no longer making decisions without the Wonderful Counselor's understanding. While in the midst of internal and external turmoil it is easy to seek advice from other believers for the answers to our situations, but God does not want us "peeking on someone else's paper." There is no

Humbly Submitting to Change

"cheating" or sharing for the "test," because they are not the *same*. We are all created differently and the order of the "test" is catered towards each individual; but think it not strange, for the fiery darts are to *strengthen* us not *destroy* us. It is the fundamental belief that God is at work in our lives and that everything is subject to His discretion. God's wisdom is not something we learn or simply something we just experience, it is received through the extracting of worldly influences that have entangled our minds and hearts. "Turn you at my reproof: behold, I will pour out my spirit unto you, I will make known my words unto you."(Proverbs 1:23) This allows the opportunity for Him to fill us with His knowledge and wisdom to fulfill *His* purpose.

WISDOM FROM ON HIGH

Only through God's wisdom can we comprehend His wonders and miracles. Our *natural* minds cannot comprehend the fact of the Red Sea being separated, the walls of Jericho falling flat, Gideon defeating His enemies with an army of only 300 men, or even fasting from food and water for 40 days like Jesus and Elijah. Every miracle in the Word of God could not be obtained with the wisdom of *men*; it is only the wisdom of the Creator of everything that can manifest wonders like those *and* greater.

Before David became king over Israel, we see that his wisdom was rooted in the heart of God. In all that he did, David always turned to God and leaned on Him for instructions. He was totally dependant on God to show him which way to go, and *in* his dependence, David received the wisdom of God; which allowed him to be prosperous in his servitude to King Saul. "And David went out whithersoever

Saul sent him, and behaved himself wisely: and Saul set him over the men of war, and he was accepted in the sight of all the people, and also in the sight of Saul's servants." (1 Samuel 18:5)

The Lord dwells among those that depend on *His* understanding and not their own. David's obedience to the ways of the Lord were so evident that even Saul was afraid of him; not because of David's wisdom, but because Saul knew that God was working *through* David in a way that he could only imagine. "And David behaved himself wisely in all his ways; and the LORD was with him. Wherefore when Saul saw that he behaved himself very wisely, he was afraid of him." (1 Samuel 18:14-15)

During his time in the wilderness, God increased David's wisdom, so that he would rely on Him in spite of all the afflictions he endured. David's faith in God *and* in the promise of becoming king of Israel was not only tried, but ultimately was strengthened by overcoming all of the attacks from his enemies. Though David was unsure of *when* God would make him king, he never overstepped the will of God with the intention of overtaking the kingdom with his own hands. His knowledge of God and the wisdom that God gave him was what carried him to his destiny. Although David had battles and afflictions that he endured, his attitude was to draw closer to God to allow God to make his paths straight. The knowledge that David had of God – being a promise keeper no matter what it looked like – gave him the opportunity to know God intimately even through the "rough" times and lasted throughout his reign as King.

Humbly Submitting to Change

Following the example of David and cleaving to the Presence of God through faith, allows us to obtain the wisdom of God that is limitless and will empower us to fulfill *our* divine purpose. It is important to know that God's wisdom correlates with our Faith. As we are taken through the wilderness, God builds a bridge that connects us to His unlimited power.

This bridge is faith; faith detaches us from common sense (worldly beliefs) and frees us to dwell in God's presence. Healing, Deliverance, Salvation, Peace and Love all dwell in His Presence; this is where miracles can take place. We must recognize that *we* can not build the bridge, but it takes *God's* infinite wisdom and power.

We can say that we believe in God and are ready to walk in His purpose, but without our Creator all that we do will never be effective in our lives. We will eventually grow stagnate in our relationship with God and the yearning of a fresh word will dry up. We must embrace our wilderness experience so that, like David, our understanding of our purpose can be rooted in the heart of God.

Encampment # 8

MOUNT SINAI

"And be ready in the morning, and come up in the morning unto mount Sinai, and present thyself there to me in the top of the mount."

Exodus 34:2

Becoming a Deliverer

"The Spirit of the Lord is upon me, because he hath anointed me to preach the gospel to the poor; he hath sent me to heal the brokenhearted, to preach deliverance to the captives, and recovering of sight to the blind, to set at liberty them that are bruised," (Luke 4:18)

God has created each one of us to be a deliverer for His people. It is His Divine Purpose for us to deliver and set free all that are bound. Jesus realizes that we can not deliver or liberate His people without us being delivered *first*. But many times we fail to comprehend the importance of the wilderness because we don't recognize the magnitude of the role we carry for our generation. Without a deliverer, our generation will continue to be destroyed through their lusts. "In those days there was no king in Israel, but every man did that which was right in his own eyes." (Judges 17:6)

Deliverance is more than just delivering a message from the Lord to His people, it requires *us* to first *partake* of the Word that has been placed in us. A deliverer has to surrender themselves to the message, in the wilderness, allowing the Word to change *them* first. We can never fully impact others to change if there is no evidence of change in *our* lives.

There is a gift in each of us that is hidden and is necessary to be revealed in us in order to set God's people free. "Neglect not the gift that is in thee, which was given thee by prophecy, with the laying on of the hands of the presbytery." (I Timothy 4:14) Many of us live ignorant to the fact that God has placed *everything* we need, *inside* of us. The *wilderness* is where we will find clarity to what gifts are in us. The world has limited our minds to think that our lives are insufficient, and so we perceive ourselves as weak and common. Our families and love ones regard *others* as special and talented, while they say that *we* are just ordinary. The comparisons of others have caused us to devalue our gifts and talents, and neglect them as we fall into vanity. The world makes us feel like we are not good enough so we strive to achieve success by imitating others that are regarded as talented. We take on a persona that hides the "real" person within and we then live under masks.

I have two sons that are complete opposites. One listens, the other does not; one helps clean, while the other is easily distracted. One <u>thinks</u> first, the other <u>acts</u> first. Even though they are completely different, they both are extremely special. Many times they both want to do the things that the other is good at, because they see the rewards and the praises that result. As they focus on things that don't come naturally to them, they begin to neglect their own gifts and their actions are ultimately in vain. Just like God does for us in the wilderness, and just as I must do for my sons, it is important that I also help reveal to them the greatness that is inside of them; making them confident in being who God created them to be.

Many of us do not understand that it does not matter what we are good at; love is showing and appreciating people for who God created them to be. Many times we are scarred because we are compared to others, instead of being appreciated for our differences. Nevertheless, we must know that it is not *us*, but the gift of God that is *in* us, that will shake our generation.

MOLDED TO DELIVER

Many of us are bound by our past experiences; we are scarred and wounded from those trials. As the heat from the wilderness penetrates our skin, the bandages that covered our wounds no longer stick to us because of the sweat that we are releasing. Our wounds now are open and we are vulnerable in the wilderness. Initially, we begin to look for things that can cover our wounds, but find no sufficient substitute. Our wounds are completely exposed before God, but this allows *Him* to begin the true healing process. In our lives we want to walk in purpose, see miracles, and see God's people delivered, but contradictorily we refuse to expose our wounds to God. When God sees our wounds, He heals them that we might be an example to others of His Power.

Those of us that God has purposed have no choice than to come to grips and admit that we need to be healed physically, emotionally, and spiritually; we have carried these scars for too long. As God takes us through the wilderness – with our scars exposed – we become emotionally detached from the hurt and pain that our past experiences imprinted on our hearts. We do not have to avoid our past, because we are no longer bound by it. Satan wants us to feel embarrassed about our past *and* present state, which literally shuts the door of growth to our future. "The thief cometh not, but for to steal, and to kill, and to destroy: I am come that they might have life, and that they might have it more abundantly." (John 10:10) We can not forget that Jesus is in control. So, no matter what we have been through or are currently going through, He has orchestrated it for our good. We need not be ashamed, for it is through our situations that we receive our testimony. "Be not thou therefore ashamed of the testimony of our Lord, nor of me his prisoner: but be thou partaker of the afflictions of the gospel according to the power of God;" (II Timothy 1:8)

Our testimonies must be heard to set free those that are still bound by Satan's lies. We are important to God and we are the chosen vessels that He is sending to deliver new wine to His people. "But the Lord said unto him, Go thy way: for he is a chosen vessel unto me, to bear my name before the Gentiles, and kings, and the children of Israel:" (Acts 9:15) There is no room for guilt, regrets, lusts and failures; we *must* make room for God's new wine to dwell in us. When others drink of His wine, they will taste what has been missing from their lives and be made whole. We must endure the wilderness not for us to be blessed, but so that others might see – through our lives – and glorify the Father through the Son. "Verily, verily, I say unto you, He that believeth on me, the works that I do shall he do also; and greater works than these shall he do; because I go unto my Father. And whatsoever ye shall ask in my name, that will I do, that the Father may be glorified in the Son."(John 14: 12-13) After Jesus has dealt with the wounds of our past we then can become equipped for our future.

WALKING WITHOUT A LIMP

Although the wounds of our past have disappeared, the wilderness is *still* necessary to break the carnal habits that we have entangled ourselves with for years. Our carnal habits will only corrupt the cord that connects us to God. "Because the carnal mind is enmity against God: for it is not subject to the law of God, neither indeed can be." (Romans 8:7) Though our ways might not be labeled as sin, *anything* we do or possess must come into agreement with God's vision and purpose for our lives. Our true identity is a *spiritual* identity which relies on us to maintain a lifestyle that is focused on satisfying the Spirit of God in us. "That the righteousness of the law might be fulfilled in us, who walk not after the flesh, but after the Spirit." (Romans 8:4)

God is ready to reveal Himself in us but our ways must inhabit His character. God wants more than just people that are applying His principles, He desires to dwell inside of us. Jesus is a God of action. He desires to work miracles and wondrous works *through* us, but more than anything, He wants to liberate His people so they can worship Him without restraints. "And thus are the secrets of his heart made manifest; and so falling down on his face he will worship God, and report that God is in you of a truth." (I Corinthians 14:25) Miracles are just the evidence that God is working through us, but the true power lies in our liberation from sin. Healing means nothing if the person that is healed refuses to give God the glory He deserves. True worship is a sacrificial lifestyle enveloped in Godly habits.

When I played football in college, I injured my ankle running a pass route in practice. It was extremely painful to the point I could not put <u>any</u> weight on it. So, the medical trainer checked it out and told me I had a high ankle sprain (which generally takes a couple of months to fully recover from, if not longer). The trainer then told me something that I find now to be so profound. He told me "Don't walk with a limp, just walk like you usually do." I thought at the time the man was crazy because the pain was almost unbearable when I put normal pressure on my ankle. His reasoning was that he did not want me to get used to the habit of limping because it would prolong my recovery. "And make straight paths for your feet, lest that which is lame be turned out of the way; but let it rather be healed." (Hebrews 12:13) Though it was painful walking normally, the pain was necessary for my ankle to regain strength and not gain any bad habits while I was injured.

In our lives we have grown accustomed to our limping so much, that our *limp* has become the "norm" in our lives. We have forgotten what it felt like to walk without limping. It becomes our crutch that we revert back to when the pain begins to intensify, and it hinders our growth. Though God has healed us, our limping habits continue to hinder us from reaching our ordered place in God. The wilderness experience can seem so unbearable and the pain excruciating, but it is necessary to walk *through* the pain so that God can strengthen the limbs of our lives, without us picking up any unnecessary habits that will prevent authenticity in our ministry.

When we limp we justify ourselves in our trials. Like some of us, a limper wants the benefits of a deeper relationship without exposing our flesh to the pain required to reap those benefits. This places us into a stale relationship with God because our actions are vain and unfruitful in His Sight. To reap our true identity, we must be crucified in the wilderness. "Knowing this, that our old man is crucified with him, that the body of sin might be destroyed, that henceforth we should not serve sin." (Romans 6:6) Our death is of the utmost importance, enabling us to free the people of God that we have been chosen to reach. We must offer ourselves as living sacrifices unto God so that He can use us at His discretion.

LIVING WITH NEW GARMENTS

Jesus is in the midst of our wilderness waiting to be reconciled with the "true" us that holds nothing in a higher regard than Him. Our Creator has called us into the wilderness to unlock who we really are inside, but we must be determined to endure the natural pain that the wilderness encompasses to reap our spiritual gain and understanding of who we really are.

The wilderness, however, forces us to unclothe ourselves of our dead layers of flesh. When the sun begins to shine on us, we overheat and have to remove the unnecessary garments that have led to us overheating. As we unclothe ourselves under the sun, we realize the stuff we have been wearing has been hiding our dirty underclothes. The more we take off, the more dirt we see, and as the sun sheds light on us, we see our self-righteousness as filthy rags. Although we would rather *skip* the undressing process, the wilderness forces us to confront ourselves and remove our clothes until we are naked before God.

Though we are naked before God, it is not enough if we are still dirty and polluted from the world. Jesus sends the rain into the wilderness to cleanse us and purify our ways from the influences of the world.

"Sow to yourselves in righteousness, reap in mercy; break up your fallow ground: for it is time to seek the LORD, till he come and rain righteousness upon you." (Hosea 10:12)

Every raindrop is sent with the purpose to eradicate us from the bad habits that have been polluting our lives. God's word can not be polluted and influenced by our carnal ways, so God unclothes us through the Word, purifies us by the Word, and then clothes us with *new* garments in the Word.

As believers we struggle to fulfill God's Will and are never set free, let alone helping anyone else be free, because God unclothes us and washes us, but then we put our *old* clothes back on. We fail to recognize our folly and still try to minister to others, but ultimately, with no true success. Wearing old clothes after we have been cleansed hides the smell of our newness from others. People will not see the change in us unless we let go of the carnal clothes and live in our spiritual garments. No matter how many good deeds we do, our righteousness is as a filthy rag. "But we are all as an unclean thing, and all our righteousnesses are as filthy rags; and we all do fade as a leaf; and our iniquities, like the wind, have taken us away." (Isaiah 64:6)

Our ways and actions can not add anything to our garments, but our new garments of Christ's righteousness shield us from the pollution of this world. Our new garments can not be purchased they must be given by God. "And I said unto him, Sir, thou knowest. And he said to me, These are they which came out of great tribulation, and have washed their robes, and made them white in the blood of the Lamb." (Revelations 7:14) It is vital as a deliverer to understand the importance of wearing our new garments and keeping our robes washed by the Presence of God. A deliverer must be set apart and arrayed in God's righteousness; for if we look like the world, our voice will be muted and our work will be vain.

Encampment # 9

TABERAH

"And he called the name of the place Taberah: because the fire of the LORD burnt among them."

Numbers 11:3

Validated by Purpose

All of our experiences in the wilderness are unique; meaning God deals with us *individually*. He knows exactly what is in our heart and creates avenues of change to produce understanding and knowledge through each experience. Without life changing experiences we will become haughty, unsympathetic *and* our ministry will never penetrate the hearts of God's people.

God desires us to live in the passion of the Spirit. Jesus' ministry was a ministry of compassion for His people. Our lives must exhibit the same intense compassion that Jesus' had. "Shouldest not thou also have had compassion on thy fellowservant, even as I had pity on thee?" (Matthew 18:33) A life of compassion is a life that invokes the spirit of change in God's people. "And of some have compassion, making a difference:" (Jude 1:22)

Our measure of success is not how much money we receive or how big our ministry has grown; it is how effectively we have liberated others to turn their hearts back to living a life consumed by the Spirit of God. So many churches and church leaders gauge their success by how financially successful their ministries are. "Which have forsaken the right way, and are gone astray, following the way of Balaam the son of Bosor, who loved the wages of unrighteousness;" (II Peter 2:15) They pacify their followers into believing that money is the answer to all of their problems.

> "These are wells without water, clouds that are carried with a tempest; to whom the mist of darkness is reserved for ever. For when they speak great swelling words of vanity, they allure through the lusts of the flesh, through much wantonness, those that were clean escaped from them who live in error. While they promise them liberty, they themselves are the servants of corruption: for of whom a man is overcome, of the same is he brought in bondage." (II Peter 2:17-19)

Our relationship with God will determine how those that follow the spirit in us will be set free from their natural and carnal minds. If our lives as deliverers are consumed by getting money, we will rob God's people from experiencing true freedom in God. The authenticity of our words comes from the confidence that God is working in the midst of our lives.

Our lives are not meant to impress others with the wisdom and understanding we have received from God. It is neither to show others how talented and blessed our ways are; our lives are at the discretion of God to do what *He* sees fit. "Being then made free from sin, ye became the servants of righteousness." (Romans 6:18)

The wisdom and authority that we receive is not of ourselves but of our Creator that has chosen to establish His Glory in us. God validates us to carry His power for the sole purpose to free His people to serve Him. We must allow God to give us an audience and a voice that invokes freedom in His people. "Then the LORD put forth his hand, and touched my mouth. And the LORD said unto me, Behold, I have put my words in thy mouth." (Jeremiah 1:9)

THE TRAP OF EMOTIONS

It is painful to see people bound by circumstances and not be permitted to share what God has revealed to us. However, we don't have the authority to choose *who* or *when* God liberates people through us. It is in God's hands so that we don't emotionally pursue things that God has not given to us. We must continually pursue the Presence of God in all that we do so we don't make the mistake of falling out of the Will of God, even though our intentions seem innocent. In the Word of God, we see Peter's emotions controlling his actions a number of times.

> "From that time forth began Jesus to shew unto his disciples, how that he must go unto Jerusalem, and suffer many things of the elders and chief priests and scribes, and be killed, and be raised again the third day. Then Peter took him, and began to rebuke him, saying, Be it far from thee, Lord: this shall not be unto thee. But he turned, and said unto Peter, Get thee behind me, Satan: thou art an offence unto me: for thou savourest not the things that be of God, but those that be of men. Then said Jesus unto his disciples, If any man will come after me, let him deny himself, and take up his cross, and follow me." (Matthew 16:21-24)

Jesus had just blessed Peter and told him that he would give unto him the keys to the kingdom. After the disciples began to learn of Jesus' coming death, Peter heard those piercing words from the Lord and he could not contain his emotions. Peter did not want his Hero to suffer and die, so he allowed his emotions to overtake him, which opened the door to being controlled by his flesh. Peter had forsaken everything he knew to follow Jesus and he could not imagine being separated from his friend. Naturally, no one wants to lose a loved one, but we can not let our feelings get in the way of fulfilling our purpose nor hindering anyone else's. Our emotions, like Peter's, can lead us astray from the Plan of God because we do not want to subject ourselves to pain.

Peter submitted himself to Jesus when everything was going good, but when Jesus began to speak about suffering, Peter wanted to take control. He got an attitude with the Plan of God; he was not going to allow his friend to subject himself to an undeserved suffering. As Peter did, we try to talk to Jesus and reason with Him, because we do not understand the path that God takes us through; we want to take back control of our lives and try to look for another way to accomplish God's purpose. Instead of surrendering to God, we surrender to our emotions, allowing our flesh to dictate our actions. Our flesh does not want to subject us to the suffering required to reap spiritual growth in God. However, we must deny our emotions and follow the Spirit of God wherever and however He leads.

SUBMITTING TO CHANGE

Our validation comes from *humbly submitting ourselves to change*. God does not want us comfortable and secure in ourselves, but rather to have our spirit open to the changes that inhabits our growth. "Woe to them that are at ease in Zion..." (Amos 6:1)

It is in the wilderness that we become desperate and driven to accomplish *God's* will not our own – even to the point of self-deprivation. We no longer are concerned about our reputations or the esteems of men and the benefits of the world; we are only concerned that God has found pleasure in us. No more are we entangled with the narcissistic words of man. If no one encourages us or supports the message that God has given us, it does not matter. It is not about their reactions good or bad; we must have confidence in knowing that *God* is in control, not *us*.

When things don't materialize as we envision them, we sometimes become confused and think that we have stepped out of God's will. We have *not* stepped out of God's will, we only need to wait on God and allow His word to run it's full course, that He might be Glorified through our lives and of those that He will set free. "Being confident of this very thing, that he which hath begun a good work in you will perform it until the day of Jesus Christ:" (Philippians 1:6) God has entrusted us with His Word and it is His divine plan for His Word to accomplish that which He desires. We can hold fast to every promise that God has given us through His word and rest assured that it is imminent. "For all the promises of God in him are yea, and in him Amen, unto the glory of God by us." (II Corinthians 1:20)

There is no way that we can overcome illness, poverty, doubt, fear, depression – let alone the wilderness – without the guarantee that God's promises are true and valid in our time of need. We must hold onto our hope that He will never leave us nor forsake us. What a God we serve; that in the midst of overwhelming odds, He still fulfills His promises to us to manifest His Glory through His people.

The word in us must carry power, power that is evident by the result it leaves. God shakes the wilderness to draw out the best in us. "The voice of the LORD shaketh the wilderness;..." (Psalms 29:8) The word in our mouth is about to shake and shape a generation; its purpose is to turn their hearts back to our Father. We must be shaken in the wilderness to receive our assurance that the word is of God and not of ourselves.

NO EXPERIENCE NECESSARY

One requirement in the church now is being qualified to minister to God's people, meaning, we need a certificate that validates that we know God. The piece of paper that a man gives you will not draw you any closer to God. "For I neither received it of man neither was I taught it, but by the revelation of Jesus Christ." (Galatians 1:12) Our validation comes from our relationship as we pour our hearts out to God with attentive ears receiving His instructions. Some Christians will not even listen to a preacher or teacher *unless* they have a bible degree; not realizing that their "qualified" preacher's relationship with God might be worse than their own.

We can have all the wisdom and knowledge that we want, but without the Spirit of God leading us and teaching us, our wisdom is *nothing*. Whatever we obtained *before* entering the wilderness is of no value *except* the Spirit of God. The *Spirit* working within us affirms what God will do in our lives, not our *education*. "Now when they saw the boldness of Peter and John, and perceived that they were unlearned and ignorant men, they marvelled; and they took knowledge of them, that they had been with Jesus." (Acts 4:13) It was the Spirit of *Christ* speaking through Peter and John that affected their adversaries. The people against *us* even have to marvel at the Spirit of God and the works He performs.

Humbly Submitting to Change

THE LORD LOOKS ON THE HEART

"And it came to pass, when they were come, that he looked on Eliab, and said, Surely the LORD's anointed is before him. But the LORD said unto Samuel, Look not on his countenance, or on the height of his stature; because I have refused him: for the LORD seeth not as man seeth; for man looketh on the outward appearance, but the LORD looketh on the heart." (I Samuel 16:6-7)

If it were up to *man*, David would have never been anointed king. Samuel took one look at Eliab and just knew he was the next king, because he was looking at how *visually* appealing Eliab was. God does not call us because of our *outward* beauty, but because He sees purpose in our *hearts* that He wants to manifest through us.

"Again, Jesse made seven of his sons to pass before Samuel. And Samuel said unto Jesse, The LORD hath not chosen these. And Samuel said unto Jesse, Are here all thy children? And he said, There remaineth yet the youngest, and, behold, he keepeth the sheep. And Samuel said unto Jesse, Send and fetch him: for we will not sit down till he come hither. And he sent, and brought him in. Now he was ruddy, and withal of a beautiful countenance, and goodly to look to. And the LORD said, Arise, anoint him: for this is he." (I Samuel 16:10-12)

Thank God our future is not up to *man*. David had been forgotten with the sheep; Samuel even had to ask if he had anymore children. David's *own* father did not even see the king in him. In life we are often overlooked, but no matter what man thinks, God is going to fulfill His divine purpose in spite of man's wisdom.

Validated by Purpose

God has anointed us and no matter how long it takes for the manifestation of His promise, we have already been anointed for kingship. David was a young man when he was anointed, but did not become king until he was thirty years old. The *validation* for his kingship came through *his* wilderness experience.

God calls us then conditions us through the wilderness; we need no man to cosign on the assignment that God has given. What God is about to do through us, no previous experience is required. "The Lord GOD hath given me the tongue of the learned, that I should know how to speak a word in season to him that is weary: he wakeneth morning by morning, he wakeneth mine ear to hear as the learned." (Isaiah 50:4) We will receive our training through the wilderness. When our journey through the wilderness is complete, we will have received everything we need to perform what God has purposed for our assignment. The more we embrace our training, the more successful we will be in our purpose. We must be diligent in the teachings of the Lord or we will fail to grasp the abundance of blessings He wants to bestow in our lives. We must overcome the wilderness to become unmovable in the midst of an unstable world.

Encampment # 10

KIBROTHHATTAAVAH

"And they removed from the desert of Sinai, and pitched at Kibrothhattaavah."

Numbers 33:16

Finding Faith

"By faith Enoch was translated that he should not see death; and was not found, because God had translated him: for before his translation he had this testimony, that he pleased God." (Hebrews 11:5)

What is your testimony? What is it that you have experienced that will sustain your faith in God? Have you overcome financial hardship? Have you overcome abuse? Has your life been subject to persecution and turmoil that you had to endure? Again, what is your testimony? Our experiences in the wilderness and how we handle them will dictate our future destinations in life. Israel murmured and complained in the wilderness, and *that* generation *never* made it to their Promised Land. (Numbers 14:27-29)

How miserable would we be if we could see our blessings but never be able to obtain them? Israel missed out on their blessings because of unbelief and the same problem of unbelief also hinders us from obtaining the fullness of God in our lives.

Satan has distorted our teachings and taken our faith and belief from *God's* Will to *I* will.

"How art thou fallen from heaven, O Lucifer, son of the morning! how art thou cut down to the ground, which didst weaken the nations! For thou hast said in thine heart, *I will* ascend into heaven, *I will* exalt my throne above the stars of God: *I will* sit also upon the mount of the congregation, in the sides of the north: *I will* ascend above the heights of the clouds; *I will* be like the most High." (Isaiah 14:12-14)

When we follow Satan, *we* become the god of our lives, *we* dictate our future, *we* follow our goals (career, family, achievements), *we* establish our legacy and *we* control our environment (financial, emotional, and physical). It is important however, that we understand we are but *dust* without the breath of God working in our lives and that we will be cut down just like Lucifer was if we continue in our own will. Many of us praise Jesus with our *mouths*, but our *actions* reveal from our hearts that we do not believe in Him. "Wherefore the Lord said, Forasmuch as this people draw near me with their mouth, and with their lips do honour me, but have removed their heart far from me, and their fear toward me is taught by the precept of men:" (Isaiah 29:13)

WHO ARE WE RUNNING FROM?

A little while ago, I had a dream that really troubled me. I was outside walking and I was being followed by someone who I thought to be Satan. I started running, but no matter where I went, he was right behind me. I did all that I knew I could do to lose him but all my efforts failed. I became desperate and tired of running so I made up in my mind, I was going to stop running and confront my pursuer. When I turned around and I looked at my pursuer, I realized that it was not Satan at all – it was *Jesus*. It was a hard truth that I had to swallow: I had been running from God. "Say unto them, As I live, saith the Lord GOD, I have no pleasure in the death of the

Humbly Submitting to Change

wicked; but that the wicked turn from his way and live: turn ye, turn ye from your evil ways; for why will ye die, O house of Israel?" (Ezekiel 33:11) I had been so comfortable with my situation and lifestyle that I failed to recognize the calling on my life. I had failed to see the wickedness that I was doing by running from God through my actions.

I had been faithful to my church and to my appointed positions but could not hear the Call of God. I began to ask: Does God know all the things that I do for Him? Is not my service and praise to Him enough? Why is He calling me to do things that I am not qualified to do? Has all my work been in vain? God do you understand me or am I misunderstood by You too? These questions sat pitted in my heart, all because I had my back to God. "And they have turned unto me the back, and not the face: though I taught them, rising up early and teaching them, yet they have not hearkened to receive instruction." (Jeremiah 32:33)

God holds all the answers and gives peace to all the doubts that lay in our hearts, but we must turn around and seek His face. We can be successful in our own strength, but it will be for naught if our hearts are not sealed with God's love. "Who hath also sealed us, and given the earnest of the Spirit in our hearts." (II Corinthians 1:22) We must not let our lives become a *service* instead of a *sacrifice* unto God. He wants to teach us and show us who we really are, but it requires a turning from all that we know or have experienced. The Holy Ghost reveals hidden gifts within our hearts; in order to get to these gifts we must be separated from the things that are entangled with our flesh and that have covered our limitless potential. These gifts can not be acquired or obtained through hard work, but they must be given directly from the hand of God.

WALK IN YOUR HEALING!!!

The current teaching of healing has been greatly diluted and unfortunately, carnally influenced. We are surrendering our promises of being healed by trusting in "common sense" to leave our faith in the hands of unbelievers (doctors, scientists, and society). Our faith in healing *must* be established in the Lord if we desire to see people set free from sickness and disease. If we want to experience divine healing in our life right now, we must turn our hearts back to God and receive the promise that He gives to those that are obedient to His voice.

> "And said, If thou wilt diligently hearken to the voice of the LORD thy God, and wilt do that which is right in his sight, and wilt give ear to his commandments, and keep all his statutes, I will put none of these diseases upon thee, which I have brought upon the Egyptians: for I am the LORD that healeth thee." (Exodus 15:26)

Is healing that easy to obtain? Yes it is, but the problem is that we'd rather keep running in our situations instead of stopping, turning and receiving the voice of God into our lives. We exert all of *our* options before we even try God, while all the time we think we are trusting God for our healing, but continuing to do things on our *own*. This is not to say that we will *never* get sick, however, if we let Him He *can* and *will* heal us. "O LORD my God, I cried unto thee, and thou hast healed me." (Psalms 30:2)

I have not always believed this way; it has taken my wilderness experiences to unlock my faith in truly believing in divine healing. Before, I had always been accustomed to

Humbly Submitting to Change

taking pills whenever I got a headache, had sinus problems, or anything that affected my body. When I had a cold, I would go to the store and get cold medicine. Anything worse, I would go straight to the doctor. At the doctor's office, and after a lot of questions, they would eventually give me a prescription – sometimes even *more* than one. I would take sinus medicine first thing in the morning, just to start my day so that I could prevent a sinus attack later on. It was never a problem, because I would rarely get sick growing up.

I was a good athlete and had good health. I could literally eat *anything* and never worry about the consequences of eating the "wrong" foods. I never had stomach problems ever in my life. My body, then, took a 180 degree turn for the worse as my relationship with God grew. My sickness caused me to go from a former-chiseled, 220-pound football player, down to a slim, 170-pound man in a matter of weeks. I was afraid because I was unsure of what was happening to me. I had always been emotionally and physically strong in my life. *I* was the one everyone else looked to for strength, but I suddenly became scared and confused and I just wanted to be back to my normal self again.

Shortly before my "transition," I got married and I hated that my wife had to see me in my "weak" state. I went to the doctor and told her all of my symptoms in order to find out what was wrong with me. My body was so withered from the sickness that the doctor was very concerned about future consequences, if I lost *any* more weight. I was told to take my prescriptions after *every* meal, as well as cut all dairy from out of my diet. She also said that this sickness was something I was going to have to live with for the rest of my life. At that

Finding Faith

time, I did not care about anything she said, as long as I could take the medicine and not suffer anymore.

I had gone from eating whatever I wanted, to the extreme opposite of being very obsessed with restricting my food intake. I was bound to my fear of going through the pain and suffering that my body had previously endured. I took medicine after each meal I ate and became addicted to the medicine because of the temporary "peace" it gave me. The problem was that the drugs only suppressed my symptoms; they never eradicated the illness from my body. As the months went by, the drugs no longer produced an effect in my body, but only *added* to my pain and suffering. I began to get angry at God for letting me suffer like that. I did not understand why this illness had befallen *me*. I felt alone in my suffering and depressed at the thought that this was my undeniable future. No one else knew how bad my situation had gotten *except* my wife, because I internalized all of my pain. Ultimately, I quit taking the medicine because it did not work; yet, I was still bound by my fears.

I struggled continuously and wavered with my faith in God for my healing until my turning point, when I read James 1:6-8:

> "But let him ask in faith, nothing wavering. For he that wavereth is like a wave of the sea driven with the wind and tossed. For let not that man think that he shall receive any thing of the Lord. A double minded man is unstable in all his ways."

I began to understand that God wanted me to *trust* Him for my healing. My prayers changed and the seed (Word from God) grew in my heart. My suffering began to feel lighter through reading and studying the Word of God. I went in the prayer line at my church many times and believed in my mind that I was healed, but my *heart* was still covered by fear.

Finally, one day I received the Word of the Lord in my *heart*, so when I got in the prayer line, I undoubtedly believed that Jesus was going to heal me completely. When we touched and agreed, I was instantly healed! *Now*, my family and I, after enduring many trials and experiences, believe in God's divine healing power and no longer subject ourselves to the bondage of fear. In sickness or in health we are unchanged in our submission to the authority of God and rest in the promises He has given us. It took one Word for me to be healed and He will do the same for all who let Him.

> "And saying, Lord, my servant lieth at home sick of the palsy, grievously tormented. And Jesus saith unto him, I will come and heal him. The centurion answered and said, Lord, I am not worthy that thou shouldest come under my roof: but speak the word only, and my servant shall be healed. For I am a man under authority, having soldiers under me: and I say to this man, Go, and he goeth; and to another, Come, and he cometh; and to my servant, Do this, and he doeth it. When Jesus heard it, he marvelled, and said to them that followed, Verily I say unto you, I have not found so great faith, no, not in Israel." (Matthew 8:6-10)

The centurion man understood the power and authority that was in the mouth of Jesus. He humbled himself before God and came with the expectation that if he could just receive a word, his servant would be healed. Many times we expect our pastors and missionaries to pray for us to receive our healing, but if we begin to reverence the words of *God* and not *man*, we will receive our healing with a great understanding of

His power. It is by the name of Jesus that we receive our deliverance.

Without going through *my* suffering I would have never known God to be a healer. Understand that God has created everything, so *medicine* is not the problem, it is *us*. Do our actions show that we are relying on Jesus to heal us or are we making decisions based off of fear and convenience?

> "And Asa in the thirty and ninth year of his reign was diseased in his feet, until his disease was exceeding great: yet in his disease he sought not the Lord, but to the physicans." (II Chronicles 16:12)

At one point in his life, King Asa relied solely on God in all that he did. (II Chronicles 14:11) However, he did not seek God in his *affliction*, but rested only in what the doctors could do for him. It was not that King Asa did not know God could deliver him, but he chose to rely on what he could do for himself. God does not want us to rely on the help of man; He wants us to rest in the strength of His Word so His Power can be seen. "For the eyes of the Lord run to and fro throughout the whole earth to shew himself strong in the behalf of them whose heart is perfect toward him......." (II Chronicles 16:9) A pill may be able to subside an illness, but God wants us to turn to Him first. When we place our hope in what *we* can do, our faith in God can not grow. We must not destroy ourselves due to the lack of faith anymore, but rather add to our faith through every experience that God takes us through, by relying on Him. "Knowing this, that the trying of your faith worketh patience. But let patience have her perfect work, that ye may be perfect and entire, wanting nothing." (James 1:3-4) We can say that God is our "all and all," but He wants us to *practice* what we preach. "The husbandman that laboureth must be first partaker of the fruits." (II Timothy 2:6) If we are to experience true and complete healing, we can not quench the Spirit with our "common sense" but rather embrace the opportunities that God gives us to stretch out our faith.

"Behold, I am the LORD, the God of all flesh: is there any thing too hard for me?" (Jeremiah 32:27) No!

How tragic it is when we go through our trying situations and don't seize the opportunity to allow God to work in our lives.

FEAR UNCOVERED, FAITH TRIED

Why are we so afraid to trust God? Why do we continually intervene and create our own paths? We are so afraid of change that we become our own biggest stumbling block. "Son of man, these men have set up their idols in their heart, and put the stumbling block of their iniquity before their face: should I be enquired of at all by them?" (Ezekiel 14:3) Fear has controlled our thoughts, actions and lives for so long it has become "common". Fear is being fed into our minds with movies, television, music, newspapers and our daily conversations with other people. Every choice we make is based off of fear. There are many churches that only use fear to draw people to salvation in God. Do we really love God or are we just scared of Hell?

Our society lives off of people making decisions based on their fears. We can't truly believe in God because we have been conditioned to worry about the "what ifs" in life. What if our car breaks down? What if we don't have money for college? What if our business fails? What if we lose our job?

Finding Faith

What if we are honest with our spouse and they divorce us? What if our child is diagnosed with a disease? What if God is not listening? What if I don't recover? What if I trust God and I die tomorrow? What if? These are just a few of the questions that fester through our minds daily. We don't realize that every thought – small or great – impacts our decisions when we allow them to dwell in our minds and not surrender them to the Holy Spirit. "Casting down imaginations, and every high thing that exalteth itself against the knowledge of God, and bringing into captivity every thought to the obedience of Christ;" (II Corinthians 10:5)

God must uncover every one of our fears and doubts in the wilderness for us to attain true faith in our Living Savior. True faith comes from experiences that have forced us to make decisions that put our natural reasoning and our faith in God to the test. Trusting God can be very hard when we are the only one that believes God will come through on our behalf. Every experience is a faith building experience; we must forsake all and commit ourselves to our Comforter, Jesus Christ.

At one point in my life, I struggled with being uncertain about my family's future. Back then, I was working a part-time job *and* running a Printing business with my wife. I knew in my heart that I needed to let go of my part-time job, but I had grown comfortable there. I was well liked by everyone and I made pretty good money. My desire was to work on our Printing business full-time, but I wanted to see major financial improvements before finally letting go of the part-time job. My wife and I started our Printing business in obedience to God, but I could not put my full energies into the business because I felt I had to "look out" for my family. My fears were that, if I left my part-time job, how could we afford to keep health insurance? We wouldn't have a guaranteed paycheck every week through our business, so how could we afford for me to quit when the bills were tight already with *both* of the incomes?

My Pastor preached a sermon about overcoming our fears and how our fears paralyze us into holding onto things that have no place in our future. He spoke that the things we hold on to, are *nothing* compared to what God wants to give us. God spoke through my pastor into my heart when he said, "you are holding onto nothing." I was so moved by those words, because I realized I had been holding on to a job that God had called me away from. I had given my fears the power over my present and future. I had been looking for a financial miracle in my life that would allow me to leave my job and work on the business, when all I needed was to let go of my cares and fears. I left my job the next day, committed myself to the business and cut all ties I had to the job. I was at peace with the decision, for I knew that it was God who made it, I just had to walk into it. That year, our business revenue increased four times more than the previous year. God is a keeper and He desires to be the only influence in our lives. What God speaks to us is not for anyone else to heed to, but for *us* to specifically obey.

CONSQUENCES OF DISOBEDIENCE

"And it came to pass, as they sat at the table, that the word of the LORD came unto the prophet that brought him back: And he cried unto the man of God that came from Judah, saying, Thus saith the LORD, Forasmuch as thou hast disobeyed the mouth of the LORD, and hast not kept the commandment which the LORD thy God commanded thee,

Finding Faith

But camest back, and hast eaten bread and drunk water in the place, of the which the Lord did say to thee, Eat no bread, and drink no water; thy carcase shall not come unto the sepulchre of thy fathers. And it came to pass, after he had eaten bread, and after he had drunk, that he saddled for him the ass, to wit, for the prophet whom he had brought back. And when he was gone, a lion met him by the way, and slew him: and his carcase was cast in the way, and the ass stood by it, the lion also stood by the carcase." (I Kings 13:20-24)

How tragic was the end of this man of God. He had just spoken a powerful word from the Lord to the corrupt King Jeroboam. However, he was not swayed by King Jeroboam's offer to eat or receive a reward, and refused both. The man of God was obedient in all that he did, but made the mistake of resting before the fulfillment of his assignment. "And went after the man of God, and found him sitting under an oak: and he said unto him, Art thou the man of God that camest from Judah? And he said, I am." (I Kings 13:14) In seeking comfort under the oak tree, the door was opened for him to disobey the word of the Lord. The man of God knew that there were no loopholes around what God had spoken to him, but he listened to the old prophet lie and died as a result of his disobedience. No matter what someone says to us – regardless if they say God has sent them or not – if we have heard God's voice, we *must* be obedient to His complete instructions or we will suffer the consequences of our disobedience.

On his journey back home, the man of God *had* to be hungry. He was instructed to speak to King Jeroboam, so his assignment made it easy for him to refuse the king's offer of food and gifts. Nevertheless, after completing his assignment, God sent him a completely different way than he was used to

Humbly Submitting to Change

traveling and was very unfamiliar to him. "So he went another way, and returned not by the way that he came to Bethel." (I Kings 13:10) Sometimes when God sends us by an unfamiliar route, we become unsure of our direction. We then begin to look for ways to preserve ourselves and doubt that the word God gave us will be enough to sustain us. In the uncertainty of our direction, someone usually comes into our lives and offers us a way out of our struggle. If we accept their offer, we lose our opportunity for God to increase our faith through the experience and we perish in the process. It is tragic to be used by God but still die because we did not completely obey His voice.

God is not a conventional God but rather an unconventional God that has called and chosen unconventional people to serve Him. The world will not understand the decisions we make, because they are *God's* decisions, not *ours*. If we don't experience the wilderness and *overcome* our fears, our faith will be *hindered* by our fears. If we have not experienced miracle healing, how can we witness to someone about divine healing? If we have never received the baptism of the Spirit, how can we teach about the Holy Ghost? God conditions our experiences and test us individually according to what our fears are. Our faith must flourish in the wilderness in order for our spiritual minds to receive the nourishment needed to fulfill our divine purpose.

Encampment # 11

HAZEROTH

"And the people journeyed from Kibrothhattaavah unto Hazeroth; and abode at Hazeroth."

Numbers 11:36

An Empty Bottle

What is in me? What truly inhabits my existence? Why do I struggle to fulfill God's purpose? Many of us fall short of God's glory because of our refusal to confront our inner man. It is too painful to find and accept that our hearts are not aligned with the Will of God, but our lives must submit to change in order to obtain a deeper relationship with God. We cannot blame anyone for the condition of our hearts. People can place stumbling blocks in front of us but our heart determines how we react to their persecution. No one's torment toward us is worst than how we torment ourselves in our own minds. We live defeated and confused lives because of the struggle in our beings with accepting the truth.

When the going gets tough, we give up on marriages, education, friends, church and *ourselves*. Where is our faith? "I tell you that he will avenge them speedily. Nevertheless when the Son of man cometh, shall he find faith on the earth?" (Luke 18:8) There is no substance or depth to our lives due to the fact that we are blinded from the power that lies within. For example, when we are not instantly successful in our ventures, we lose hope, admit we made a mistake and say that the venture was not in God's will. We don't like our flesh to be exposed to the chilling glare of our unhappy spouse. We

An Empty Bottle

even try to avoid having to experience being excited about a worship service and we end up being the only one that shows up.

Will we throw in the towel when there is not enough money to pay the utility bills and buy groceries for our family? Will we give up on God when our lives seem to be getting worse? It is easy to serve and worship God when our lives are settled and we have no wants or struggles. Is that a prosperous life, though? Are we successful when we are exempted from tribulations and persecution? What substance will we have to ourselves if we never go through anything? Yes, from the outside we might have it all together, but our insides are empty and dormant. God refuses for His people to live hollow lives.

SPIRITUALLY EMPTY

God does not want us to be visually appealing while our divine purpose does not produce fruit for His people.

> "And Jesus entered into Jerusalem, and into the temple: and when he had looked round about upon all things, and now the eventide was come, he went out unto Bethany with the twelve. And on the morrow, when they were come from Bethany, he was hungry: And seeing a fig tree afar off having leaves, he came, if haply he might find any thing thereon: and when he came to it, he found nothing but leaves; for the time of figs was not yet. And Jesus answered and said unto it, No man eat fruit of thee hereafter for ever. And his disciples heard it. (Mark 11:11:14)

Just as the fig tree, sometimes our outward appearance is beautiful and the people of God are drawn to us to eat of the fruit from our branches. Unfortunately, they come to us but we have nothing to satisfy their hunger. We have not yielded any

Humbly Submitting to Change

good fruit because we have concentrated on feeding our *outward* appearance. If we can not feed God's people His good fruit, then our lives are in vain. "Every tree that bringeth not forth good fruit is hewn down, and cast into the fire." (Matthew 7:19) We can look the part, but if we are not willing to sacrifice our beauty to nourish the hungry we will be dried up by the Son. "And in the morning, as they passed by, they saw the fig tree dried up from the roots." (Mark 11:20)

We must focus on our purpose, which is feed to the hungry, the fruit of God. People will want us to take on titles that have not been given by God and duties He has not ordered, but it is our responsibility to reject any assignment except if it has been given by Him. We will lose our sweetness and our fruit will be corrupted because it will not be connected to its source. "And the trees said to the fig tree, Come thou, and reign over us. But the fig tree said unto them, Should I forsake my sweetness, and my good fruit, and go to be promoted over the trees?" (Judges 9:10-11)

Every hollow person, when exposed, is vulnerable to being filled with the carnal things of this world. Though on the outside we are perceived to be honorable and holy, our inside is being destroyed by the seeds of this world. In the midst of the storm, the seeds that have been planted in us will begin to spurt on the outside. No matter how much we hide what dwells within, it will eventually come out, given the right situation.

> "Whosoever cometh to me, and heareth my sayings, and doeth them, I will shew you to whom he is like: He is like a man which built an house, and digged deep, and laid the foundation on a rock: and when the flood arose, the stream beat vehemently upon that house, and could not shake it: for

it was founded upon a rock. But he that heareth, and doeth not, is like a man that without a foundation built an house upon the earth; against which the stream did beat vehemently, and immediately it fell; and the ruin of that house was great." (Luke 6:47-49)

The "flood" is coming no matter if we are doing the will of God or not. It is up to us to determine what our result will be when the flood comes. The worldly things that have filled us can not be mixed with God's Spirit; there must be a discharge of the carnal things so that we can be filled with the fullness of God. Our lives must be poured out before God with no residue of the old inhabitant.

This is an agonizing process because it takes the act of letting go of everything – nothing is exempted. "… let us lay aside every weight, and the sin which doth so easily beset us, and let us run with patience the race that is set before us," (Hebrews 12:1) Our freedom lies in us letting go of our control and walking in what God has already promised.

BROKEN OLD BOTTLES

Do we really want to be filled by God? To be filled we must first be emptied. To be empty requires us to change from our normality. The issue that we often struggle with is that change is always painful to our flesh that has grown comfortable in our regular routine. For example: when we begin to use joints that are not accustomed to exercising, they easily become fatigued and sore. The body hates to subject itself to pain because if grows comfortable with being stagnant. The same thing happens when we ask God to change us and fill us with His Spirit but we don't fully comprehend what we are asking for.

Humbly Submitting to Change

> "Neither do men put new wine into old bottles: else the bottles break, and the wine runneth out, and the bottles perish: but they put new wine into new bottles, and both are preserved." (Matthew 9:17)

We ask God to empower us and fill us, but we still live as "old bottles." When God fills us with new wine, we become broken; His Spirit then spills out of us and we perish. As we continue to hold on to our old ways, lives, emotions, fears and relationships, we remain an old bottle and we become broken by the Presence of God. God wants to fill us but He is not the problem we are.

> "Woe unto you, scribes and Pharisees, hypocrites! for ye make clean the outside of the cup and of the platter, but within they are full of extortion and excess. Thou blind Pharisee, cleanse first that which is within the cup and platter, that the outside of them may be clean also. Woe unto you, scribes and Pharisees, hypocrites! for ye are like unto whited sepulchres, which indeed appear beautiful outward, but are within full of dead men's bones, and of all uncleanness. Even so ye also outwardly appear righteous unto men, but within ye are full of hypocrisy and iniquity." (Matthew 23:25-28)

We avoid cleaning the inside of our lives because it first requires pouring out the vain contents and washing our lives from the crude of self. "Wash you, make you clean; put away the evil of your doings from before mine eyes; cease to do evil;" (Isaiah 1:16) We only clean the outside of our lives so that people can see that we are holy. While we appear to be "new bottles," we still hold on to our old contents.

When we are empty, we are hungry for something to fill us. So, we are afraid of dying from starvation and we hate

An Empty Bottle

feeling that we have no control over our situations. The issue is not that we don't believe in God, we just don't want to endure the effects of our hunger. Our bodies can not handle the overwhelming infilling of the Holy Ghost. It can't possibly contain the slightest bite of the Spirit without us becoming broken.

When God imparts His Spirit in us, He shows us our place in Him and our blinded eyes are open to the corruption in our hearts. Yes, we have been faithfully serving at our church, paying our tithes, involved in volunteer work and we never miss a Sunday morning service. Still, there is something missing; our hearts are not in it. "For do I now persuade men, or God? or do I seek to please men? for if I yet pleased men, I should not be the servant of Christ." (Galatians 1:10)

We have failed to keep God in the midst of our hearts because we are busy trying to serve Him our *own* way. We become frustrated and burned out from our involvement in so many ministries, that we lose sight of God's vision and we "check out". We do the work, but our hearts are lost and empty of passion. Our feelings have overshadowed our purpose, and the people that are in need perish, because of our selfishness. Our lives have become dry and we look for ways to get out of our rut. We become desperate for change and want God to revive our spirit again. "Create in me a clean heart, O God; and renew a right spirit within me." (Psalms 51:10) When God touches us, our broken hearts are filled with sincerity and the people around us are blessed because God's love flows through us. "…the bottles break, and the wine runneth out…" (Matthew 9:17)

Humbly Submitting to Change

There is nothing like the feeling that comes upon us when God touches our heart; we then sincerely praise Him with no restraints. God loves to fill our hearts; He delights in the praises of a contrite spirit. "....I dwell in the high and holy place, with him also that is of a contrite and humble spirit, to revive the spirit of the humble, and to revive the heart of the contrite ones." (Isaiah 57:15) The problem is that the feeling does not last. We shout on Sundays with our hearts broken before God and our services yield many spiritual blessings of joy. We are blessed by the Presence of God and our brokenness allows the Spirit to touch the hearts of others – but we still perish!

"...the bottles break, and the wine runneth out, and the bottles perish..." (Matthew 9:17)

We are addicted to the *feeling* of being filled, but are not ready to allow God to create us into a new vessel. We don't carry any substance for our lives or for God's people because our broken vessels have emptied the new wine it was carrying. We have become addicted to a *feeling*, but not to the Fullness of God. God is seeking a vessel that He can dwell in continually; a vessel that is built by the incorruptible Word of God and that is cleansed through submission to His Will. "Being born again, not of corruptible seed, but of incorruptible, by the word of God, which liveth and abideth for ever." (I Peter 1:23)

UNDER CONSTRUCTION

Let us not fool ourselves from the reality of our current state; we are under construction. We don't know what God has next for us – all we see is chaos. We understand God has a purpose for our lives but are confused on how he is going to turn our "mess" into His masterpiece. Though our situation is out of our control, we submit ourselves to *God's* plan. We empty our carnal thoughts and they are replaced with the Word of God. God wants to "check in" and work in our lives.

Our construction is reliant on our submission to God. We must see our end before we begin. "But Christ as a son over his own house; whose house are we, if we hold fast the confidence and the rejoicing of the hope firm unto the end." (Hebrews 3:6) It is easy to submit to the good things in life but our attitudes must remain the same even when the tribulations ravish our lives. When we are pressed and squeezed, we learn what is inside of us. What comes out of us is determined by what is poured into us.

TEMPTED IN OUR WEAKNESS

Our emptiness leaves us vulnerable to the temptations of the devil. "Watch and pray, that ye enter not into temptation: the spirit indeed is willing, but the flesh is weak." (Matthew 26:41) We are presented with choices that will determine who will fill us. The devil desires to fill us with the fears and cares of this world, so that we will not be able to handle our journey through the wilderness.

When we are weak and empty, our flesh desires things that are not good for us. When I am hungry, instead of wanting a meal, I crave snacks. I go to the grocery store without eating at home first and by the time I am ready to check out, I am hungry. I want something that is going to satisfy me until I eat my meal. I buy the conveniently-placed snacks by the checkout lines and consume them before I even leave the

Humbly Submitting to Change

parking lot. Though they are delicious, they only intensify my hunger and on top of that, it also unsettles my stomach.

Spiritually, we do the same thing; we are in so much of a hurry to prepare a feast(ministry) and gather all the necessary ingredients(gifts needed for ministry) that we forget to eat breakfast(our daily appointments in the Presence of God, Devotion) before we go to the store. Initially, we feel we will be okay because we don't feel hungry. We proceed in obtaining our ingredients as we focus are time and energies on getting what we want. After we have gathered all the necessary items we get in line to pay for them (we must understand there is a cost to serving God). When we consider the cost, we realize that we are hungry (empty) because we have skipped our meal (time with God) and we look to what is placed in front of us to fill our void. We are already in line and we look to see what we can get that will satisfy us *now*. We are hungry, so we are not picky on what we intake as long as it will take away the feeling of an empty stomach.

Our temptations have been strategically placed in front of us. They are the things that taste delicious but are not good for an empty stomach. So, we can either decide to get a snack or wait to eat our meal at home. Many times we choose to get the snack because we allow our empty stomachs (flesh) to decide. The snacks curve our appetites, but now our stomachs are unsettled (we suffer for yielding to our temptations).

As our thoughts and lives are consumed and filled with moving in our gifts and purpose, we deprive ourselves from our meals (daily devotions at the feet of Jesus) and our relationship with God becomes shaky. Our passion to pursue

An Empty Bottle

the Presence of God is curved when the temptation has upset our empty vessel and separated us from our purpose.

If we yield to our flesh we will be filled with fleshly desires, if we yield to the Spirit we will be filled with spiritual desire for God's Presence. It is not enough to surrender to being emptied by God; we must patiently wait for God to fill us, so that we can fulfill our divine purpose. "Blessed is the man that endureth temptation: for when he is tried, he shall receive the crown of life, which the Lord hath promised to them that love him." (James 1:12)

Encampment # 12

WILDERNESS OF PARAN

"And afterward the people removed from Hazeroth, and pitched in the wilderness of Paran."

Numbers 12:16

Submitting to Change

What is our motivation? I remember watching and laughing at a *Sprite* commercial when the actor said, "Excuse me, excuse me what's my motivation?" At the end of the commercial they would say, "Obey your Thirst." What are we truly thirsty for? We must be conscious to what thirst we are obeying. Have you ever tasted something that you could never get enough of? Our flesh craves to eat more of it, and is determined to satisfy our craving, no matter what. "Hell and destruction are never full; so the eyes of man are never satisfied."(Proverbs 27:20) We all may have different tastes, but we all are craving *something*. It may be attention from people or perhaps we are craving money; regardless, we must recognize what it is that we are thirsty for.

Our problem is that we have forgotten what the presence of *God* tastes like. "O taste and see that the LORD is good: blessed is the man that trusteth in him." (Psalms 34:8) We have confused our thirst for His presence with a thirst for attention, riches, security, and earthly prosperity. We want His "Blessing Plan" but are not thirsty enough to dwell in His Presence. We don't crave the presence of God because we are comfortable obeying our fleshly thirst. Many of us starve our spiritual man, as we crave and ultimately satisfy our carnal

Submitting to Change

desires. We even become fearful of the presence of God due to the fact that His presence invokes change in our lives. His Presence exposes our positions and our lifestyles; we can't enter His Presence and remain the same.

> "And he went thither to Naioth in Ramah: and the Spirit of God was upon him also, and he went on, and prophesied, until he came to Naioth in Ramah. And he stripped off his clothes also, and prophesied before Samuel in like manner, and lay down naked all that day and all that night. (I Samuel 19:23-24)

Saul was filled with evil indignation towards David. His pride drove him to Naioth because he could not understand why his orders were not being carried out. So, he took on the mindset that he would handle David himself. "Therefore pride compasseth them about as a chain; violence covereth them as a garment." (Psalms 73:6) Saul was so focused on killing David, that he ignored the pride that disconnected him from God. "The wicked, through the pride of his countenance, will not seek after God: God is not in all his thoughts." (Psalm 10:4) Regardless if his messengers could not fulfill his orders, he was determined not to let even *God* get in his way from satisfying his desire to kill David.

Saul traveled to Naioth with evil intentions, but God had His *own* intentions for Saul. When the Spirit of God came upon Saul, the power of God's presence overwhelmed him. God "hit" Saul so hard that he stripped off his clothes in God's presence and remained naked before Him all day.

When we begin to act as Saul and disregard the pride that is within us, our comfort is replaced with discomfort and our happiness is replaced with lowliness. "When pride cometh, then cometh shame: but with the lowly is wisdom." (Proverbs 11:2) In our lowliness, we find Christ and He purges our carnal desires, enabling our eyes to open and see ourselves clearly. When we realize that our actions have separated us from God we become low in our regard of ourselves.

SPIRITUALLY OUT OF SHAPE

I can recall once when my church was having prayer meetings everyday for about four months. I felt that I was progressing in my spiritual walk and that I had a great understanding of what God wanted to do with me. "Be not wise in thine own eyes: fear the LORD, and depart from evil." (Proverbs 3:7) My family went faithfully to the prayer meetings and God's Presence would fill the room and my heart daily. The only problem was that I would sweat out my clothes, and by the end of prayer, I would stink. Everyone else was fine; they did not sweat or stink, it was just me. No matter what I did, the same thing would happen every time, and people started to avoid me after prayer. While I was praying, I asked God, "Why do I sweat so profusely?" God spoke as clear as day and said to me, "You are spiritually out of shape."

He revealed to me in that moment that I had polluted my body with the cares of this world. The sweat was God's way of purging me of all the impurities that I had sown into my body. The smell was the scent of the toxic poisons that were destroying my inner being; the smell of sin and disobedience has a horrible stench. "My wounds stink and are corrupt because of my foolishness." (Psalm 38:5) I became so overwhelmed by His words that I could only cry out to Him.

Submitting to Change

Before the prayer meetings even began, I had no prayer life. I only sincerely prayed to God in my times of dire need. However, at those meetings I embraced an intimacy with my Father. I yearned to hear a Word from Him, which gave Him the opportunity to teach my heart. "The Lord GOD hath opened mine ear, and I was not rebellious, neither turned away back." (Isaiah 50:5) When I entered God's Presence I realized that I was not as close to Him as I thought. Nevertheless, God's desire was to show me my place in Him.

God can change us with just one Word. In my communion with Him, God impregnated me with purpose and a desire to fulfill His will. "That he no longer should live the rest of his time in the flesh to the lusts of men, but to the will of God." (I Peter 4:2) God had to shake me to show me I was not where He wanted me to be and my sweating was necessary for me to be stirred to change.

STATE OF LOWLINESS

"But what things were gain to me, those I counted loss for Christ. Yea doubtless, and I count all things but loss for the excellency of the knowledge of Christ Jesus my Lord: for whom I have suffered the loss of all things, and do count them but dung, that I may win Christ," (Philippians 3:7-8)

Paul's past and all of the accolades he had, were of no value to him compared to the relationship he had with God. He lost everything after his conversion at the price of fulfilling his divine purpose in God. In losing everything that profits our flesh, we become free in our spirit to pursue God.

Being in a low condition, gives us opportunities to try God and stand on His Word. We can not make provisions for ourselves when our lives are out of our control, but it does not

Humbly Submitting to Change

matter, for we have nothing to lose. A servant does not decide his own assignment, but only can fulfill what He is asked to do. Everyday, we have to ask God for our assignment, we must not assume we understand His plan but rather surrender to His will daily. Our hearts must yield to His love and instruction or we will fail by mistaking His voice for our *own*. We fail God when we murmur against His plan. "Wherefore doth a living man complain, a man for the punishment of his sins? Let us search and try our ways, and turn again to the LORD." (Lamentations 3:39-40)

We don't understand why *we* have to be lowly, while everyone *else* is being exalted. It seems like everyone sees the gifts in others, but we are invisible, going unseen and hidden from the world. "But let it be the hidden man of the heart, in that which is not corruptible, even the ornament of a meek and quiet spirit, which is in the sight of God of great price." (I Peter 3:4) God's hands are working in our lives. He has hidden us from the world so that when He is ready to use us, we will remain invisible, causing Him to get all of the glory. If everyone immediately recognized our gifts, they would fail to see *God's* power working through us. He desires for our lives to be invisible so that His light might shine *through* us and ultimately draw His people back in communion with *Him*.

In humbling ourselves, we become armored through our weakness.

> "But they that wait upon the LORD shall renew their strength; they shall mount up with wings as eagles; they shall run, and not be weary; and they shall walk, and not faint." (Isaiah 40:31)

Submitting to Change

When we are alone with God, He delivers us out of the paws of a lion and a bear, so that we may be equipped to slay giants in our spiritual journey. We have no means of saving ourselves; our lives are completely in the hands of our Deliverer.

The world sees our plight and is judgmental of our relationship with God. They ask questions like: *"Is it God's Will for you to be poor?"* *"Is it God's Will for you to be sick?"* They do not understand that without us going through our circumstances, we could never be a witness of God's delivering power. Yes, it *is* God's will for me to be poor, so that He can deliver me out of the paws of poverty. "This poor man cried, and the LORD heard him, and saved him out of all his troubles." (Psalms 34:6) Yes, it *is* God's will for me to be sick, so He can deliver me out of the paws of disease. "Bless the LORD, O my soul, and forget not all his benefits: Who forgiveth all thine iniquities; who healeth all thy diseases;" (Psalms 103:2-3)

In each experience we are weak, which gives God the chance to be strong in us. Our lives are then armed with the knowledge of God's ability to deliver us out of *any* situation. In our desperate situations, we are made whole and complete for our divine purpose. In our solitude with God, He is able to unlock the hidden treasures within us.

FITTING INTO GOD'S PLAN

Are we complaining or are we content with His placement? "Not that I speak in respect of want: for I have learned, in whatsoever state I am, therewith to be content." (Philippians 4:11) When we submit ourselves to His divine

Humbly Submitting to Change

placement for our lives, we will be unchanged by our circumstances. We will not be moved and distracted by money or poverty, but only by the Spirit of God. We might not understand our purpose, but when our hearts are submitted to Godly change we will yield wisdom that is immeasurable to the world. God is looking for us to be a willing vessel that is going to allow Him to place us into our ordained position. "For we are his workmanship, created in Christ Jesus unto good works, which God hath before ordained that we should walk in them." (Ephesians 2:10)

It might not be what *we* had envisioned for our lives, but it is what God has *created* us to do. God's plan is to align us with our purpose so that we properly fit in His Body. Individually, we can be gifted. However, if we are out of place on our "team," we will prevent the body of Christ from achieving Victory. Our role is *key* and vital to achieving victory in our homes, communities, and churches.

We have been filled with so much pride by our society, that we don't know how to be a good "team" player. "The pride of thine heart hath deceived thee, thou that dwellest in the clefts of the rock, whose habitation is high; that saith in his heart, Who shall bring me down to the ground?" (Obadiah 1:3) Through our pride, our marriages are being destroyed, churches are being divided and communities are now war zones, because we have failed to permit God to place us into position. We are out of balance because *we* have determined our *own* positions. No one is being healed, no one is being set free, and no one is changing; we are too proud to admit that *we* are the problem. It is easier to ignore our pride "issues" than to submit to change.

Submitting to Change

When we heed to the instructions of God, the name on the *front* of our "team" jersey is more important than the name on the *back*. We will embrace the "team" and concentrate on our own job. Doing that, will allow our teammates to focus on their jobs and make victory imminent, for we then will be playing as one. Pride brings dissention, but a humble heart creates a direct avenue towards the presence of God. Our lives are of no use if they are not properly fitted in the Body of Christ.

THE SECRET OF STILLNESS

We have been created for kingship but we *must* learn how to be still and find rest in our alone time with God in order to obtain our crown. It is through our *humility* that God is honored, and through our *silence*, we learn our place in God. In our stillness, we honor God because instead of being our *own* hindrance, His Spirit is allowed the chance to work on our behalf.

We must commit ourselves to stillness, for it is the key to experiencing the miracles and promises of God. It is very challenging to submit ourselves to stillness because it forces us to let go of the reins and place our lives in God's complete control. We have such a strong urge to do something about our situations, so we can feel we are making progress. It is hard for us to just stand and not intervene in our own lives.

> "And when they had sent away the multitude, they took him even as he was in the ship. And there were also with him other little ships. And there arose a great storm of wind, and the waves beat into the ship, so that it was now full. And he was in the hinder part of the ship, asleep on a pillow: and they awake him, and say unto him, Master, carest thou not

Humbly Submitting to Change

that we perish? And he arose, and rebuked the wind, and said unto the sea, Peace, be still. And the wind ceased, and there was a great calm. And he said unto them, Why are ye so fearful? how is it that ye have no faith?" (Mark 4:36-40)

The disciples could not understand how Jesus could be sleep while in the midst of such a great storm. Their fears provoked them to ask Jesus, "...carest thou not that we perish?"

They lost hope in God because they were so consumed in dealing with the element they were in. When our "ships" become full of water, our flesh begins to question why Jesus is "sleeping." Does He not see that we are about to drown in our problems? Jesus had just spoken parables to the multitude *and* expounded on the meaning to His disciples, but when that same word should have given them peace in the sea, they instead became offended by their circumstance. "And have no root in themselves, and so endure but for a time: afterward, when affliction or persecution ariseth for the word's sake, immediately they are offended." (Mark 4:17)

Jesus found comfort in the midst of chaos. He was resting on a pillow while his disciples were troubled by the storm. Like the disciples, we wait for our ships to be full of water *before* we wake up Jesus with our cries. We act on our fears, and when it seems the situation is about to destroy us, *then* we call on Jesus. God wants us to rest in Him; no matter day or night, rain or shine, He wants our minds focused on Him. Jesus trusted in the Word. He slept on the Word *and* He calmed the winds and the sea through the Word. If we are resting on our pillow – the word of God – we will be covered by God's peace and not be affected by our trying situations.

God has promised us peace; all He asks from us is that we *allow* His peace to work through our lives. "LORD, thou wilt ordain peace for us: for thou also hast wrought all our works in us." (Isaiah 26:12)

In stillness we also learn of God's character. We receive clarity in our situation which permits growth and change in us. Our tempter wants us to fret and be anxious in our decisions, but God is calling for us to be still so that we may know Him as our God. When we concede to our flesh we become restless and anxious for immediate results. Our results are that we fall deeper into our messes and become separated from our divine assignments. God has placed everything we need inside of us to accomplish our assignments, but we need to be *still* to receive His divine instruction.

EMPOWERED BY STILLNESS

Can God trust us with His treasures? If God placed a million dollars in your hands today, but told you not to spend it until His instruction, would you wait on Him? Or, would you take control of the blessing that is in your hands? God has placed spiritual "treasures" in our hands, but He wants to give us instructions on how to effectively use them. Our tempter does not want us to receive any instructions; he wants us to be ignorant and immediately use what we have been given. We are tempted to embrace and display our gifts, but we have no clue on how we are to use them. How many times will we have to start from the beginning before we read the instructions? Our gifts can only benefit us when they are properly operated in the way they were designed to be used. Our lives will continue to be filled with fears and uncertainties when we ignore the process of stillness. We will know God's

Humbly Submitting to Change

way and His plan for us when we patiently wait on His instructions. "The LORD is good unto them that wait for him, to the soul that seeketh him." (Lamentations 3:25)

In our stillness, we acknowledge God's greatness and we are at peace in our condition. Our stillness sets us apart from tradition and rituals; it liberates us from the limitations that our carnality has placed on our lives. Stillness saturates us in the Presence of God. Our appetite is filled with the good seeds of God, our eyes are fixated on His pleasures, and He is attentive to our needs. In the natural sense, we have not eaten for days, but we are so filled – spiritually – by His Words that our lives and focus have shifted from "self" to God. There is a price to being filled with the Word of God, which is many great "storms." However, when we humbly stand still, we see that the storms are necessary for our growth and it allows God's Word to fulfill its purpose.

> "For as the rain cometh down, and the snow from heaven, and returneth not thither, but watereth the earth, and maketh it bring forth and bud, that it may give seed to the sower, and bread to the eater: So shall my word be that goeth forth out of my mouth: it shall not return unto me void, but it shall accomplish that which I please, and it shall prosper in the thing whereto I sent it." (Isaiah 55:10-11)

Encampment # 13

KADESHBARNEA

"Likewise when the LORD sent you from Kadeshbarnea, saying, Go up and possess the land which I have given you; then ye rebelled against the commandment of the LORD your God, and ye believed him not, nor hearkened to his voice."
Deuteronomy 9:23

Loving God

"A new heart also will I give you, and a new spirit will I put within you: and I will take away the stony heart out of your flesh, and I will give you an heart of flesh." (Ezekiel 36:26)

The love of God is so amazing; it breaks barriers and changes our stony hearts to a heart of flesh. God's love is immeasurable in our lives, and at some point in time, we have all taken for granted His Grace. In our darkest moments God's love shines the brightest and His Hands are always extended to embrace us. No matter if we fail, He is there to teach us and chasten us. "As many as I love, I rebuke and chasten: be zealous therefore, and repent." (Revelations 3:19) The question is not: *Does God love us?* It is: *Do we love Him?*

It is in our wilderness where Heaven seems so far away and we must come to grips with how much we really love Him. Our knowledge of what is in our heart will determine how long or even *if* we will leave the wilderness. As our lives are flooded with desperate situations, God is looking at our hearts to see if we will love Him in spite of the trials. He wants to see if we will turn our back to Him and go back to our "Egypt" (old sinful life of bondage). "This is he, that was in the church in the wilderness with the angel which spake to him in the mount Sina, and with our fathers: who received the lively oracles to give unto us: To whom our fathers would not obey, but thrust him from them, and in their hearts turned back again into Egypt," (Acts 7:38-39)

LOVING GOD

We must each ask ourselves if we love Him. If we do love Him, why do we fall short of His Glory? "And I will bring you into the wilderness of the people, and there will I plead with you face to face. Like as I pleaded with your fathers in the wilderness of the land of Egypt, so will I plead with you, saith the Lord GOD." (Ezekiel 20:35-36) In the wilderness, we *learn* how to love God the way He *wants* us to love Him. When we are honest with God, it allows us to commune with Him face to face, and that is where *true* intimacy begins. No longer do we have to be ashamed of our shortcomings, but can surrender our weaknesses to Him, so that the holes in our hearts can be filled.

Many of us are afraid to be honest because it makes us vulnerable and we don't want God to see all the "dirt" in our hearts. We cause pain and suffering to our loved ones because we are not honest with God. God is no fool; He just wants us to confess the truth out of our mouths so that we become conscious of our fleshy actions. If we would only see that our honesty with God frees us from wandering, it can place us on the path to change.

We are all aware of the fact that it seems easier to *lie* about touchy subjects than it is to tell the *truth*. Why is it easier to destroy ourselves than preserve ourselves? We must be honest with God to be delivered from our hardened heart. Although we may be scared of God's reaction to what lies deep within our hearts, it is necessary for us to be liberated from all the guilt that torments us and keeps us from drawing closer to Him.

OUR WALL FALL FLAT

God is gracious and merciful, but *we* must take the first step for us to *receive* His grace and mercy in our lives. This process is truly difficult because our hearts are fortified like Jericho.

> "Now Jericho was straitly shut up because of the children of Israel: none went out, and none came in." (Joshua 6:1)

Our walls are guarded and protected as we hide from our vulnerability inside. Our hearts are inhabited by fear and selfishness, and are protected by our pride. We refuse to let down our guard without a fight. God is on the outside, desiring to conquer our hearts and destroy every evil agent that festers inside our walls. Jesus has gathered His host, as the Ark of the Covenant (His presence), is carried around our walls. We believe, however, that there is no way Jesus and His army is going to conquer our hearts for we are *well* equipped for battle.

We boast, in pride, that our walls have *never* been breached and we are confident that our secrets and our sins will never be discovered. As Jesus and His host march around our walls, we don't understand their tactics, but they continue to march around us silently. "And Joshua had commanded the people, saying, Ye shall not shout, nor make any noise with your voice, neither shall any word proceed out of your mouth, until the day I bid you shout; then shall ye shout." (Joshua 6:10) The silence summons the presence of God and empowers their cry. Has Jesus ever cried out to you? When

Loving God

He has completely surrounded us, He cries out for us and our walls fall down flat.

> "So the people shouted when the priests blew with the trumpets: and it came to pass, when the people heard the sound of the trumpet, and the people shouted with a great shout, that the wall fell down flat, so that the people went up into the city, every man straight before him, and they took the city." (Joshua 6:20)

Our hearts are purged from evil and only His love remains. (Joshua 6:21) God is crying out for our hearts; He is calling out to His sheep to be reconciled with Him, their shepherd.

Our love must be rooted in *who He is, not in what He does*. Our love for Him is based on the belief of who He is. "And we have known and believed the love that God hath to us. God is love; and he that dwelleth in love dwelleth in God, and God in him." (I John 4:16) Pure love is shown not through the abundance of tangible blessings we receive, but rather, through the overwhelming knowledge of who God reveals Himself to be.

God's love is unchanged by our circumstances; it is more than an observable blessing, His love *is* the blessing. No matter how we *perceive* Him, He is unquestionably who He *reveals* Himself to be. Unfortunately, our love is fickle towards God. "And because iniquity shall abound, the love of many shall wax cold." (Matthew 24:12) We love God as long as He blesses us with health, provisions and even salvation, but when things are taken away, we turn our hearts from God and look for the comfort of someone or something else.

BE NOT OFFENDED

"Now when John had heard in the prison the works of Christ, he sent two of his disciples, And said unto him, Art thou he that should come, or do we look for another?" (Matthew 11:2-3)

John was bound in prison and heard of the works that Jesus had done, but in his affliction, he questioned if Jesus was the Christ. John *knew* Jesus was the Christ, but while in his turmoil, he started to doubt. Just as John, we sometimes do not understand the process that God takes us through and we begin to doubt His plan for our lives. We become offended by our sufferings and it hinders God's love from blessing us in the midst of our affliction.

"And blessed is he, whosoever shall not be offended in me." (Matthew 11:6)

Israel is a great example of how we can suffer because of our ignorance of God's love. As long as Israel was reaping the benefits of the power of God like manna from heaven, water from a rock and deliverance from their enemies, they freely worshipped God. Sadly, when they were hungry and starved, not only did they quickly turn their hearts away from God and complain, they also began to distrust His promises to them. So many times we have been overjoyed by what God was doing for us in our lives. At the same time, when the scent of a storm came, our countenance changed and we too began to question God's ways.

PURE LOVE

We find a perfect example of what our love should be towards God through the lives of Hananiah, Mishael, and

Loving God

Azariah. They had been taken from their country, placed in a culture that was full of many idols and false gods, and their names were changed from honorable names to names of dishonor. They were taken from everything they knew and believed in, but the *one* thing the Babylonians could not change was their *hearts*. Their hearts were yielded to serving God, and they became highly favored by the Lord in the sight of the king.

A decree was made in the kingdom for all the inhabitants to follow, but Shadrach, Meshach and Abednego refused. Their response to the decree was different from everyone else's, for all the others heeded to the warning of the fiery furnace because of their fear of death. The people conspired against them and presented them before the king for judgment; Shadrach, Meshach and Abednego were fearless, because they knew who God was and what He was able to do.

> "Now if ye be ready that at what time ye hear the sound of the cornet, flute, harp, sackbut, psaltery, and dulcimer, and all kinds of music, ye fall down and worship the image which I have made; well: but if ye worship not, ye shall be cast the same hour into the midst of a burning fiery furnace; and who is that God that shall deliver you out of my hands? Shadrach, Meshach, and Abednego, answered and said to the king, O Nebuchadnezzar, we are not careful to answer thee in this matter. If it be so, our God whom we serve is able to deliver us from the burning fiery furnace, and he will deliver us out of thine hand, O king. But if not, be it known unto thee, O king, that we will not serve thy gods, nor worship the golden image which thou hast set up." (Daniel 3:15-18) Wow!

They did not stop at their refusal to bow; even if God did not come to their rescue, it was not going to change their love (devotion) to Him. They had completely surrendered their lives to the discretion of God. *That* is the love that we must exhibit towards our Father.

Are we willing to die for our relationship with Jesus even if Heaven is not promised? Will we serve God even though our circumstances remain the same or get worse? When we exhibit sacrificial love back to God, He intervenes in a mighty way. When He is done, we don't look like what we been through; not even a slight of bit of evidence remains from the situation we have overcome.

REFINED BY FIRE

As our adversaries bind us and throw us into the fiery furnace, they don't realize that they are throwing us right into the presence of God. "For our God is a consuming fire." (Hebrews 12:29) The "fire" is exactly where God wants us to be, so that *He* can loose our binds and set us free.

> "And these three men, Shadrach, Meshach, and Abednego, fell down bound into the midst of the burning fiery furnace. Then Nebuchadnezzar the king was astonished, and rose up in haste, and spake, and said unto his counsellors, Did not we cast three men bound into the midst of the fire? They answered and said unto the king, True, O king. He answered and said, Lo, I see four men loose, walking in the midst of the fire, and they have no hurt; and the form of the fourth is like the Son of God." (Daniel 3:23-25)

We should never be afraid of the "fire," for it is *God*. Spite the fact that our adversaries thought the fire would destroy us; it rather delivered us into the Presence of God. Our faith is tried in the fire and God is magnified through the fire. We should never fight against the binds of persecution or adversity but embrace the opportunity to meet Jesus and to be freed through His consuming fire.

As we fall down in His presence, it allows God to raise us up from out of our situations and walk right along side Him. When we are completely surrendered to God, His love will meet us in our extreme situations and consume the things in us that are not like Him. Through purging our souls, only His love remains and we are able to walk *in* His Love.

> "And it shall come to pass, that in all the land, saith the LORD, two parts therein shall be cut off and die; but the third shall be left therein." (Zechariah 13:8)

In the midst of God's consuming fire, our bodies and minds can not enter into the Presence of God, only our hearts will remain. So that, when our hearts are refined and tried by God, He can mold them into His image. Then His love will shine forth through us, for then, we will be created through the purity of His fire. Whenever we shall call on Jesus, our shepherd, He will hear us and commune with us.

> "And I will bring the third part through the fire, and will refine them as silver is refined, and will try them as gold is tried: they shall call on my name, and I will hear them: I will say, It is my people: and they shall say, The LORD is my God." (Zechariah 13:9)

His love for us is so amazing, that He goes to great lengths for us to be able to dwell in His presence and live. Others will then see the goodness of God and glorify Him *as* God, all because we surrendered ourselves to the fire of God. The world looks at the "fiery furnace" and is afraid of its power, so they heed to the warnings of men and worship their works. *We* must embrace every opportunity to fall down into

Humbly Submitting to Change

the fire of God, for *that* is where we will be changed and set free.

The fire does not accomplish what our adversaries intended for it to accomplish, for the fire does not *destroy* us, it *empowers* us. There is no evidence that we were ever bound in the fire and they would never believe what God has taken us through, if they had not seen it with their own eyes. "...saw these men, upon whose bodies the fire had no power, nor was an hair of their head singed, neither were their coats changed, nor the smell of fire had passed on them." (Daniel 3: 27) They will praise God because we yielded our bodies to God and not to anything us. "Then Nebuchadnezzar spake, and said, Blessed be the God of Shadrach, Meshach, and Abednego, who hath sent his angel, and delivered his servants that trusted in him, and have changed the king's word, and yielded their bodies, that they might not serve nor worship any god, except their own God."(Daniel 3:28)

Through the yielding of a willing vessel, many miracles of God will be accomplished because *that* willing vessel is not afraid to be filled with His fire. We must yield ourselves now, to His fire, while there is a purpose for our lives. Otherwise, we will be subject to His condemning fire when He comes back.

> "As therefore the tares are gathered and burned in the fire; so shall it be in the end of this world. The Son of man shall send forth his angels, and they shall gather out of his kingdom all things that offend, and them which do iniquity; And shall cast them into a furnace of fire: there shall be wailing and gnashing of teeth. Then shall the righteous shine forth as the sun in the kingdom of their Father. Who hath ears to hear, let him hear." (Matthew 13:40-43)

SURRENDERING TO HIS LOVE

When we have surrendered to His fire, we are elevated by the power of God. "Then the king promoted Shadrach, Meshach, and Abednego, in the province of Babylon."(Daniel 3:30) God rewards those that love Him for who He is.

> "But without faith it is impossible to please him: for he that cometh to God must believe that he is, and that he is a rewarder of them that diligently seek him." (Hebrews 11:6)

Our love must be unchanged no matter what the problem or situation is; we must never yield ourselves to anyone other than *Jesus*. In the midst of God's fire, our bodies and souls become submitted to His Spirit that is *in* us. We can never get to the same love the three Hebrew boys had, if our bodies and minds are not yielded to what our refined hearts are ready to accomplish.

We must know Him *intimately* if we are to completely trust and surrender to His will. As God empowers our spirit through His Word, our bodies and minds become aligned with our divine purpose, and we can then productively love God the way He has *commanded* us to.

> "And thou shalt love the LORD thy God with all thine heart, and with all thy soul, and with all thy might" (Deuteronomy 6:5)

God has called and chosen us by His love, but through His refining fire, our bodies and souls are purged from the pollution of this world that has clouded our judgment. "Behold, I have refined thee, but not with silver; I have chosen thee in the furnace of affliction. For mine own sake, even for mine own sake, will I do it: for how should my name be polluted? and I will not give my glory unto another." (Isaiah 48:10-11) Our bodies and souls fall under subjection to the spirit within, as we are constructed carry out the orders of our Creator. "...shall we not much rather be in subjection unto the Father of spirits, and live? For they verily for a few days chastened us after their own pleasure; but he for our profit, that we might be partakers of his holiness. Now no chastening for the present seemeth to be joyous, but grievous: nevertheless afterward it yieldeth the peaceable fruit of righteousness unto them which are exercised thereby." (Hebrews 12:9-11)

LIVING IN HIS LOVE

Then, with our whole being, we will honor God because we will be committed to His will. God reverses the order of priority in the wilderness, from Body – Soul – Heart, to Spirit – Soul – Body; this way, our reactions to life will always exude His love and not our selfishness. We run into trouble when we revert back to our natural order and act on our fleshly desires. When we yield to God's spiritual order, our lives are controlled by Him and our emotions are at ease. "For to be carnally minded is death; but to be spiritually minded is life and peace." (Romans 8:6)

Our love for God can *only* grow when we stay committed to the original path that God has created for us. No matter how big or small the decision, we have to surrender to the love of God, so that we will be aligned with His will. Our unconditional love for God is established through our commitment to stay faithful to His will, through better *or* worse. Keeping our vows to God is *fundamental* to us living victoriously while in communion with Him. "Ye shall walk after the LORD your God, and fear him, and keep his commandments, and obey his voice, and ye shall serve him, and cleave unto him." (Deuteronomy 13:4) In the wilderness, our spiritual man has to leave our mother and father – our natural (sin) and carnal (iniquity) lives (Psalms 51:5) – and cleave to our spouse – Jesus Christ.

> "Therefore shall a man leave his father and his mother, and shall cleave unto his wife: and they shall be one flesh." (Genesis 2:24)

It is during our honeymoon that we become intimate with God and join together to become *one*. As our relationship with Him grows, we become inseparable and His commitment to us is insured by the Word of God. "Heaven and earth shall pass away, but my words shall not pass away." (Matthew 24:35)

Our commitment is insured by our submission to His will and our love is seen through our submission to Him. When situations occur, we cast our cares to *Him* and not *"our father or mother"*. "Casting all your care upon him; for he careth for you." (I Peter 5:7) *"Our father and mother"* are not submitted to God. When we consult *them* instead of our spouse, we give *them* authority in our lives and become submitted to *them*. We *must* forsake all others so that God – our spouse – can be the spiritual Head of our household. Only *God* can protect us, only *He* can provide, only *He* can comfort us, only *He* can guide us, only *He* can love us the way we need to be loved. Our constant submission to God's authority shows Him our love and respect for His presence. In return, He overwhelms us with gifts and blessings, and is attentive to our *every* need and want.

Humbly Submitting to Change

It is *crucial* that we stay submitted to His plan so that we don't fall back into the many snares of the devil. Our dedication to God leads to a constant flow of change in our lives that will consume our hearts with the love of Christ and we become fashioned from the inside out. We no longer focus on arraying our bodies, but our hearts before God. As our hearts become fashioned to please *Him*, our minds receive peace and our bodies receive beauty.

Encampment # 14

MOUNT HOR

"And the children of Israel, even the whole congregation, journeyed from Kadesh, and came unto mount Hor."

Numbers 20:22

God's Heart

When our lives are aligned with the spirit of God, we learn to focus on the task at hand: pleasing the heart of God. To please God, we must first find *where* His heart is. God's heart is a heart yielded to serving His people. It is not a heart concerned with its *own* needs, but one that sacrifices its strength to help strengthen others. When *we* yield to the service of God's people, our hearts are filled with compassion for the ones we serve.

Our servitude is not through the busyness of legalism or religion, but through the simplicity of using the gifts He has placed in our hearts. We please God when we use what He has given us in the way that He desires us to. So, where are His teachers and writers and worship leaders? Where are His evangelists and ministers that have His heart? Who is teaching our youth the way to God? "Teaching us that, denying ungodliness and worldly lusts, we should live soberly, righteously, and godly, in this present world;"(Titus 2:12)

FEED MY SHEEP

We can not allow the pollution of this world to distort our way. When we are in the Master's hands, we don't have to preserve ourselves and make provision for ourselves; we should be serving others, whether or not they have a way of repaying us. Our focus should not be about reaching the masses, but simply pleasing the heart of God.

We have grown so focused and comfortable in our churches, our conferences and our concerts, that we have *ignored* the ones He has *called* us to reach. Where are His lost sheep? "My people hath been lost sheep: their shepherds have caused them to go astray, they have turned them away on the mountains: they have gone from mountain to hill, they have forgotten their restingplace." (Jeremiah 50:6) Where is the good pasture that they might eat and live? We can not ignore the heart of God – His people – anymore. We must feed God's sheep so that they might be nourished up and be able to recognize the call of their Shepherd.

> "So when they had dined, Jesus saith to Simon Peter, Simon, son of Jonas, lovest thou me more than these? He saith unto him, Yea, Lord; thou knowest that I love thee. He saith unto him, Feed my lambs. He saith to him again the second time, Simon, son of Jonas, lovest thou me? He saith unto him, Yea, Lord; thou knowest that I love thee. He saith unto him, Feed my sheep. He saith unto him the third time, Simon, son of Jonas, lovest thou me? Peter was grieved because he said unto him the third time, Lovest thou me? And he said unto him, Lord, thou knowest all things; thou knowest that I love thee. Jesus saith unto him, Feed my sheep." (John 21:15-17)

Just as Peter, we feel that God *knows* we love Him, because we boldly proclaim His words to all that will listen to us; we express our love to God the best way we can. So, how can God ask us if we love Him? We are *so* busy trying to justify our love for God that we ignore the mandate that He has called us to fulfill.

God is telling us that if we love Him, we will not ignore the needs of His sheep. Will we sacrifice our beauty so that they might eat? Is their life of lesser value than ours? Have we forgotten who has kept us and fed us? When we are connected to the heart of God, we have need of nothing and through *His* abundance we are able to also yield fruit for His people. *God wants to array us so that His sheep will be drawn to Him* and eat of His fruit. Only *His* fruit can satisfy their souls; we are just the branches of God that He uses to give shade to the lost and bear fruit for the brokenhearted.

A LIFE OF SACRIFICE

What is God's will for us? In order to fulfill God's will, our lives *have* to be sacrificial.

> "I beseech you therefore, brethren, by the mercies of God, that ye present your bodies a living sacrifice, holy, acceptable unto God, which is your reasonable service. And be not conformed to this world: but be ye transformed by the renewing of your mind, that ye may prove what is that good, and acceptable, and perfect, will of God." (Romans 12:1-2)

We can fulfill the law through our obedience, but to fulfill the covenant of grace, there has to be a *sacrifice*. We ask, what can we sacrifice that is of any value to God? It is the daily sacrificial offering of our hearts that He wants. Our hearts have to be yielded to His love.

Jesus is ignored everyday when we ignore the domestic violence in our homes, the violence in our streets, the children that are going hungry and the homeless that go unheard. Why do we continue to ignore Jesus? Have we sacrificed our time for Him in an unusual way or are we a product of our daily routine? Do we have enough of His Heart to allow Him to heal the lameness in our lives? God wants to work miracles in and through our lives, but we *must* meet Him where His heart is.

OPEN TO DIVINE APPOINTMENTS

Some of the most amazing moves of God that I have experienced were not in a church, but in divine appointments that God had placed in my life. We work *so* hard to garner the presence of God to fall at our church services, but it is when we are not even looking for God, that He shows up in a mighty way. I have realized that it is not enough just to praise God to reach the depths of His heart, but to seek Him in *everything* because He reveals Himself through the most unattractive situations.

I can remember one time when I was dropping off the students in our church's tutoring program. I had to rush back to church to attend an important meeting. Anyone that *really* knows me knows that I hate to be late more than *anything*. I am very controlled in trying to make sure that I am on time for my responsibilities.

As I was exiting the freeway, I noticed that the exit ramp was backed up because someone's car had stalled. When the traffic light turned green, cars just went *around* the stalled car. When I approached the car I had an attitude because I knew I was going to be late for church. As I began to go around the stalled car and saw that the owner was desperately trying to push his car out of the way, God spoke to my heart and instructed me to help him. Has God ever spoken to your heart in the midst of your busyness?

When I pulled over, I helped the gentleman who was still trying to move his car but he could not do it with his own

Humbly Submitting to Change

strength. We ended up pushing the car into an empty parking lot. He was thankful for the help and as I was about to leave him with his car, (so that I could hurry to the church meeting), God spoke to my heart again and told me, "Ask him if he needs a ride somewhere." Of course I asked, but I questioned God saying within myself: "What about church?"

As I drove the man to his destination, he began to tell me about his struggle with his relationship with God and how he was at a crossroads in his faith in God. He began to ask me questions, and the spirit of *God* began to speak into *both* of our lives. God began to use me and share things about the man through me that only He would have known. As the presence of God filled the car, strongholds in *both* of our lives began to come down. In that car ride, I saw Jesus like I *never* saw Him before.

Before his car stalled, the young man was on his way to a church bible study that a friend urged him to come to. He told me that when the car stopped on him, he was scared because he was in an area across town from where he lived. He had no means to contact his friend at the church and he felt that his situation was hopeless. Then, at his lowest point, he prayed and God told him not be afraid because help was on the way. So, he waited and then *I* showed up. As he got out of the car to enter into the church, I was awestruck at the power of God, to be able to use me even when I was not looking to be used. We were *both* headed to church and we were both detoured, so that we could meet Jesus, and *forever* have our lives impacted by His visitation. "Thou hast granted me life and favour, and thy visitation hath preserved my spirit." (Job 10:12)

Through divine appointments we find the heart of God and are forever changed by His presence. We do not have to *find* people to minister to; our lives just have to be open to the spirit of God so that He can place us in our rightful position, allowing His grace to touch His sheep. Our divine appointments are never convenient to our daily routine; they completely mess up our agenda and schedule. God wants to use us, but we have to be willing to disregard *our* agenda for *His* agenda when He calls on us.

BUSY OR OPEN

Is your line of communication busy when Jesus calls? Or, is your line open for His instruction? God is calling us, but we are unaware to His calling because our "line" stays busy. We are so consumed with our families, church, friends, television, internet, business, ministries and schooling, that our lives are *completely* filled up and we can't fit God into our schedule.

People are hurting, starving, scared *and* alone, and we are too blinded by our busy lifestyle to help them. We only help people when it is convenient for *our* schedule. God is not asking for us to disregard the things He has placed in our lives, but He does want our lives to always be open to His heart. He is calling for us because He has a work for us to do; we must be willing to answer His call and be ready for His instruction. "... And who then is willing to consecrate his service this day unto the LORD?" (I Chronicles 29:5)

Our flesh is comfortable maintaining our repetitive schedule, but our spirit is always open and ready for a change of plans. In the times that we are not looking to change and we

Humbly Submitting to Change

are secure in ourselves, *that* is when God calls. He wants us to always be eager and prepared to scrap our ways in order to be used to touch the hearts of men. *Our* work will always lead to death for us *and* the people we are trying to help.

> "Many will say to me in that day, Lord, Lord, have we not prophesied in thy name? and in thy name have cast out devils? and in thy name done many wonderful works? And then will I profess unto them, I never knew you: depart from me, ye that work iniquity." (Matthew 7: 22-23)

We don't want to look back and see that we prayed in His name, fed the poor and were consumed with meeting the needs of people, but we never *knew* God in all that we did. Our *efforts* are not what God desires. We will *only* know the heart of God when we allow Him to have our *hearts*. His heart wants to feed the hungry, heal the sick, regulate minds, and comfort the depressed. He just needs an open and willing vessel that will not hinder His love from reaching the hearts of His people.

> "If ye be willing and obedient, ye shall eat the good of the land:" (Isaiah 1:19)

Encampment # 15

MOUNT ABARIM

"And the LORD said unto Moses, Get thee up into this mount Abarim, and see the land which I have given unto the children of Israel.

Numbers 27:12

God's Eyes

"No man, when he hath lighted a candle, putteth it in a secret place, neither under a bushel, but on a candlestick, that they which come in may see the light. The light of the body is the eye: therefore when thine eye is single, thy whole body also is full of light; but when thine eye is evil, thy body also is full of darkness. Take heed therefore that the light which is in thee be not darkness. If thy whole body therefore be full of light, having no part dark, the whole shall be full of light, as when the bright shining of a candle doth give thee light." (LUKE 11: 33-36)

What are we captivated by? What are our eyes fixated on? We have grown so accustomed to seeing in the dark, that our eyes have become sensitive to light. The darkness has blurred our vision of what our reality is. Our eyes have distorted our future and have stained our past; they see no hope for our tomorrow and no purpose for our yesterday. Our eyes are never satisfied, but always looking for *more*. In the midst of the darkness everything seems to look good, but only when the light shines, is it possible to see things as they truly are.

There is no other body part that fights against our faith like our eyes. To the world, *seeing is believing*, but to God, *believing* is *seeing*. Our eyes define everything to us; from what physical beauty is, to what clothes are attractive. Our eyes even determine how we feel and guide us in what we want and desire. However, we can not appreciate the beauty of the things God has placed in front of us, when we remain blurred by our carnality.

Our children, spouses and love ones are all taken for granted because we are distracted by our selfishness. We don't appreciate the good qualities in our love ones because we are fixated on our lusts of this world. God's vision invokes peace in our homes and lives but *our* eyes produce dissention and heartache. Seeing through God's eyes takes our focus off of ourselves and places it on what *He* values as important: His love for His people. Our families, children and others need to see *His* love, not *our* wrath. Our lives must be surrendered to the vision of God for them to find Christ.

SEEING THROUGH HIS EYES

God understands the discord our eyes can cause from fully trusting in Him. We will never see God for who He is as long as our vision is blurred by our darkness. We must rely on God to be our eyes and discern what path that we are to take. "And I will bring the blind by a way that they knew not; I will lead them in paths that they have not known: I will make darkness light before them, and crooked things straight. These things will I do unto them, and not forsake them." (Isaiah 42:16)

Our trust in God *has* to be secure; for we can not live without His eyes guiding us or else we will stumble. God has extraordinary things in store for our lives, but we can not obtain His promises with our natural eyes for they can never believe in spiritual things. *Our* eyes have to be burned from

Humbly Submitting to Change

dead works for us to see God's work through *His* eyes. "But the natural man receiveth not the things of the Spirit of God: for they are foolishness unto him: neither can he know them, because they are spiritually discerned." (I Corinthians 2:14)

Though our natural eyes see destruction drawing nigh, *spiritually*, we can see how God's word is working in our lives. Our beliefs are not based on the conditions that we *see*, but on the knowledge of who God *is*. "For God, who commanded the light to shine out of darkness, hath shined in our hearts, to give the light of the knowledge of the glory of God in the face of Jesus Christ." (II Corinthians 4:6) When our eyes are burned by the Son, it is only what the Son sees that remains.

In our situations, *our* eyes see death, but *God's* eyes see life.

> "And she went, and sat her down over against him a good way off, as it were a bow shot: for she said, Let me not see the death of the child. And she sat over against him, and lift up her voice, and wept. And God heard the voice of the lad; and the angel of God called to Hagar out of heaven, and said unto her, What aileth thee, Hagar? fear not; for God hath heard the voice of the lad where he is. Arise, lift up the lad, and hold him in thine hand; for I will make him a great nation. And God opened her eyes, and she saw a well of water; and she went, and filled the bottle with water, and gave the lad drink." (Genesis 21:16-19)

Hagar saw no hope for her situation, she was afraid to see her son die. God is faithful to deliver us, but we can not allow our eyes to make us fearful. Hagar had to arise out of her fear and hold on to her purpose which was to raise her son. When she arose out of her fear it allowed God to open her eyes to God's provision which enabled her to nourish her son. Even in the midst of their lowest moment, they received a promise of life that opened Hagar's eyes to hope and provision.

"...I will make him a great nation..." (Genesis 21:18)

We have to rely on God even when our natural eyes are consumed with unbelief. Our eyes are attacked to distort our image of God and His power, which separates us from our divine purpose. We are visually stimulated and aroused by the things of this world, but God wants to be the apple of our eyes.

"Keep my commandments, and live; and my law as the apple of thine eye." (Proverbs 7:2)

Do we really find the Word of God attractive? Or has it just become a pillow to us, being read only when we are in desperate need of comfort? Our eyes must be fixated on God if we are to overcome the temptations that our eyes will be drawn to. "Watch and pray, that ye enter not into temptation: the spirit indeed is willing, but the flesh is weak." (Matthew 26:41) As men and women, we tend to search for things that will stimulate us *visually*. We are addicted to watching our favorite television show or favorite sports team. We become "locked in" to games or shows as they absorb our full attention. Even after the television goes off, we can not stop thinking or talking about what we saw.

No matter what tempts us, we have to be purged from the lusts that our eyes imprint in our lives. We become bound by the longings of our eyes; we organize our day around our favorite television show or sports game and place our lusts for the pleasures of this world in front of our desire to seek God. "But every man is tempted, when he is drawn away of his own lust, and enticed. Then when lust hath conceived, it bringeth forth sin: and sin, when it is finished, bringeth forth death." (James 1:14-15) Our lives will never bear God's fruit as long as our eyes are fixated on the things of the world. "And the cares of this world, and the deceitfulness of riches, and the lusts of other things entering in, choke the word, and it becometh unfruitful." (Mark 4:19)

TURN ON THE LIGHTS

God "turns on the lights" to show us what *and* who we are communing with. Nevertheless, it is painful for us to see the blemishes and flaws of our pleasures. In my college days, I would go to a party and dance all night with someone. There could be plenty of beautiful girls there, but the lights were dimmed down low. I liked what I saw in the dark, but when the lights came on at the end of the party, my "beauty" was really no "beauty" at all, and I was ashamed to even be seen with them. Have you ever misinterpreted things in the dark to be beautiful then felt ashamed by your poor judgment later?

God does not want us to "party" in the *dark*, but rather in *His* light. He wants us to recognize what is of Him and what is not. He is not come to end the "party," but to illuminate our lives to see the beauty of His glory and direct us to the *right* "party." So many times we act on what we see, but God wants us to rest in His image. If we can see God, we will not be separated from Him by our lusts but will be captivated by His love. When we see *Jesus*, our eyes are enlightened to the beauty of His holiness. The more we see Him the more we want to be like Him. We are no longer attracted to the person we see in the mirror; we want to see the beautiful image of *Jesus*, not *ourselves*. When we are freed from our natural eyes, our eyes are then opened to the hidden mysteries of God and we can see God's Word as He sees it. We are not drowned by our lusts but guided by His vision to change our lives.

ILLUMINATED PURPOSE

"And Jesus said, For judgment I am come into this world, that they which see not might see;....." (John 9:39)

"And he cometh to Bethsaida; and they bring a blind man unto him, and besought him to touch him. And he took the blind man by the hand, and led him out of the town; and when he had spit on his eyes, and put his hands upon him, he asked him if he saw ought. And he looked up, and said, I see men as trees, walking. After that he put his hands again upon his eyes, and made him look up: and he was restored, and saw every man clearly. And he sent him away to his house, saying, Neither go into the town, nor tell it to any in the town." (Mark 8:22-26)

When Jesus healed the blind man, he took him *out* of the city. God takes *us* away from what we have always known as well. If we are not separated from our comfort *first*, then we will want to remain in the state that Jesus found us in. God is leading us out of our comfort, which has blinded our spiritual discernment and blocked His vision from manifesting itself in our lives. God has to take us out of our "town," because what He is about to do in our lives, our love ones will not understand and can potentially hinder the work of God.

God must get us *alone*, to show us His glory. When He "spits" on our eyes to enable us to see, we can only see men as trees (carnally). Still, as we *respond* to God's calling, He touches us again and we see the way we were created to see (spiritually). Are we desperate enough to see spiritually? Will we allow God to spit on our eyes? Are we satisfied with seeing carnally or are we going to seek after His vision for our lives? He has constructed us to see spiritual things, but has to cleanse our eyes so that we can walk in the *light* and not in the darkness of *carnality*.

God is giving us His vision so that He can shine His light into the hearts of men. "Let your light so shine before men, that they may see your good works, and glorify your Father which is in heaven." (Matthew 5:16) Jesus is the *true* light and He wants to shine the beauty of His countenance through our lives. Our divine purpose has to be guided by God and not our carnal eyes if we are to *effectively* fulfill His plan.

When we see through His eyes nothing is more attractive than His image. Even the pleasures of this world are not our focus, but *are* relative to what God has in store for us. After He has equipped us with His eyes, the Spirit *in* us can discern what the will of God is *for* us. We are no longer confused as to what He wants us to do nor are we pessimistic of what our future has in store.

His eyes lead us deep into submission to His plan for us; we are completely filled and saturated by His light. With His eyes all things that He gives us are pure. "Unto the pure all things are pure: but unto them that are defiled and unbelieving is nothing pure; but even their mind and conscience is defiled." (Titus 1:15)

We are not regulated by the corruption of "self" and this world, but we thrive on the ability to see God and see through His eyes in the midst of any situation. Our eyes are liberated from the obscurity of vanity and open to the possibilities that God has placed before us. Through God's eyes, we see that He can move mountains and change the course of our futures. God will straighten our crooked paths and unlock the doors to our change. God has not called us to discern with *our* eyes and knowledge, but rather submit our eyes to *His* mighty hand so that He can conquer the impossibilities of our present and future.

God has placed His greatness deep within our hearts and He wants to unleash His greatness into our lives, so that His light can be seen throughout the world. "That ye may be blameless and harmless, the sons of God, without rebuke, in the midst of a crooked and perverse nation, among whom ye shine as lights in the world;" (Philippians 2:15)

BLINDED FOR LIFE

"… and that they which see might be made blind. And some of the Pharisees which were with him heard these words, and said unto him, Are we blind also? Jesus said unto them, If ye were blind, ye should have no sin: but now ye say, We see; therefore your sin remaineth." (John 9:39-41)

So many times we are going the wrong way. We are very successful and passionate about what we are doing in our lives. Yet, the problem is that we are ignorant to the fact that our actions are sadly destroying us. Take for instance, Saul, who was a persecutor of the early church. Saul had a part in the slaughter against the disciples of the Lord.

"And Saul, yet breathing out threatenings and slaughter against the disciples of the Lord, went unto the high priest, and desired of him letters to Damascus to the synagogues, that if he found any of this way, whether they were men or women, he might bring them bound unto Jerusalem. And as

Humbly Submitting to Change

he journeyed, he came near Damascus: and suddenly there shined round about him a light from heaven:" (Acts 9:1-3)

God shined His light on Saul for it was time for Saul to meet who he was persecuting. Thank the Lord, that He shines His light on us when we are going astray! So many times we feel that we are doing the right thing, like Saul did, but we are making our assumptions in ignorance. We are led by our desire to control our situations.

Saul was very intelligent and a scholar. When the doctrine of Jesus was being preached, it caused Saul to feel vulnerable and unsure of his own beliefs, so He attacked anyone that was teaching anything contrary to what *he* knew. Unfortunately, many of us are lost in our pride to stay who we are, but God takes the time to shine on us so that He can use us.

"And he fell to the earth, and heard a voice saying unto him, Saul, Saul, why persecutest thou me?" (Acts 9:4)

It is amazing that in the search for comfort and fulfillment in life – the God that Saul had been studying about, the God that we are curious about but can not see – reveals Himself and we cry out to Him.

"And he said, Who art thou, Lord?" (Acts 9:5)

We *want* to know who God is, but it takes *God* to shine His light on us for us to recognize His existence. We have been so consumed in darkness that when God appears, we fall down and ask, "Who are you God?" God answers us and says,

"… And the Lord said, I am Jesus whom thou persecutest: it is hard for thee to kick against the pricks." (Acts 9:5)

God's Eyes

We have been fighting against the divine calling on our lives because we have been focused on trying to serve God in the darkness. God does not want us to serve while we are blind and ignorant to His presence. We have made our lives so burdensome because we have selfishly tried to pursue God on our own terms, but when God speaks, we listen as Saul did. "And he trembling and astonished said, Lord, what wilt thou have me to do? And the Lord said unto him, Arise, and go into the city, and it shall be told thee what thou must do." (Acts 9:6)

We are in awe while in the presence of God and all we can say is: "What wilt thou have me to do Lord?" Saul had finally met the God he had always been studying, and *now* He was ready to do what He wanted him to do. Saul was not concerned about what other people thought, all he wanted to know was what he could do for the Lord; *that* is a spirit of a true servant. We have all gone astray at some time in our relationship with God, but when we are in the presence of God, our pride is blinded and our hearts are opened to His instructions.

When God tells us that He will instruct us, we have to wait until He comes to visit us. We are no longer seeking to satisfy our hunger or our thirst, but we are patiently waiting for God to speak to us. Food and drink could not satisfy Saul's desire to hear from God.

"And he was three days without sight, and neither did eat nor drink." (Act 9:9)

Three days is a long time to go without our eyesight. Some of us can not even go to sleep without a light on, so to be without our vision for even a small period of time, can be very troubling. God was preparing Saul for *ministry*. God did not want Saul to serve Him with his *own* eyesight, but rather, only through the power of *His* eyes.

In that place of solitude, God worked on Saul and prepared him to be baptized. Being alone, Saul had to think about all the evil things that He had done to God's people. He *had* to regret all the things from his past, but he just waited and held on to the promise that God was going to come and instruct him. Nevertheless, in this time of prayer and fasting, Saul had to cast all his cares and insecurities to God. "… Saul, of Tarsus: for, behold, he prayeth," (Acts 9:11)

He had to let go of his *past* and seek after the voice of God for his *future*. God desires to do great things in us *no matter* what we have done in our past; He regards our destiny. "… Go thy way: for he is a chosen vessel unto me, to bear my name before the Gentiles, and kings, and the children of Israel:" (Acts 9:15)

We are like Saul, for God has chosen *us* to bear His name and be witnesses of Him. We are *nothing* without God and we have to accept all that comes with bearing His name.

> "For I will shew him how great things he must suffer for my name's sake. And when Ananias went his way, and entered into the house; and putting his hands on him said, Brother Saul, the Lord, *even* Jesus, that appeared unto thee in the way as thou camest, hath sent me, that thou mightest receive thy sight, and be filled with the Holy Ghost. And immediately there fell from his eyes as it had been scales: and he received sight forthwith, and arose, and was baptized." (Acts 9:16-18)

The scales over our eyes then become our past; we are no longer bound by our past regrets and we can see through

God's Eyes

God's eyes. We are blinded for life because we are under the will of *God*, not *our* will. We are blinded to our ways and free to live the life God has called us to live. "And straightway he preached Christ in the synagogues, that he is the Son of God." (Acts 9:20) As we walk in our purpose, people will be amazed at our transformation. They will remember our past ways and be in awe at what God is doing through us.

> "But all that heard him were amazed, and said; Is not this he that destroyed them which called on this name in Jerusalem, and came hither for that intent, that he might bring them bound unto the chief priests? But Saul increased the more in strength, and confounded the Jews which dwelt at Damascus, proving that this is very Christ." (Acts 9:21-22)

We must be blinded from our ways in order to receive our true life's purpose that God has called us to fulfill.

Encampment # 16

PLAINS OF MOAB

"And they departed from the mountains of Abarim, and pitched in the plains of Moab by Jordan near Jericho."

Numbers 33:48

God's Life

"As for me, I will behold thy face in righteousness: I shall be satisfied, when I awake, with thy likeness." (Psalms 17:15)

God wants us to experience *true* life in Him. God's spirit quickens our dry bones and we are awakened to His plan for our lives. Our lives are enjoined with God's purpose, which then endows us with the power to change. God's life is a life of *change*. Every moment in the presence of God brings a new *change* into our lives.

"One thing have I desired of the LORD, that will I seek after; that I may dwell in the house of the LORD all the days of my life…" (Psalms 27:4)

Our one desire each day should be to dwell in the presence of God, who inhabits the praises of His people. Our lives should be consumed with seeking God's face. We have not been created just to occupy space, but to awaken God's people to the calling of our Savior. We don't have time to relive the regrets of our past; neither do we have the strength to handle the trials of our future. The *one* thing we can do is rest in the Holy Spirit in our *present*.

"Brethren, I count not myself to have apprehended: but this one thing I do, forgetting those things which are behind, and reaching forth unto those things which are before," (Philippians 3:13)

LIVING FOR TODAY

When we live in the Spirit *today*, we are freed from all of our regrets and cares and are empowered to "seize the day" in order to live life to its fullest.

> "I press toward the mark for the prize of the high calling of God in Christ Jesus." (Philippians 3:14)

In the Spirit, our lives can not be ruined by the wounds that others have inflicted on our lives; each day, our lives are cleansed of yesterday and our activity is rested in submission to God's Will. We become yielded to the needs of the people that *Jesus* wants to impact for the day. We are all constructed differently and we must embrace our differences so that we may effectively change the course of men; God wants to use our lives to align His people back to their rightful positions.

> "And the LORD said unto Samuel, How long wilt thou mourn for Saul, seeing I have rejected him from reigning over Israel? fill thine horn with oil, and go, I will send thee to Jesse the Bethlehemite: for I have provided me a king among his sons." (I Samuel 16:1)

How long will we dwell in the past? We must seize the moment and be filled with the anointing of God because He wants to use us to anoint His people into His Kingdom. His Spirit must flow through us and conquer the hearts of His people so they can be anointed for His service. Through yielding our lives to God, whomever He has called, will recognize His voice and change their ways. "Verily, verily, I say unto you, The hour is coming, and now is, when the dead

Humbly Submitting to Change

shall hear the voice of the Son of God: and they that hear shall live." (John 5:25)

Everything we need is in us; we just have to yield our lives to *Jesus* to find what we are seeking for. So many times we are afraid to submit ourselves for we think our lives will be dry and boring, or we are scared to change for we fear that we won't like who we will become. We see all the benefits to a deeper relationship with God, but we are not sure if it is worth the daily battle to surrender our will in exchange for God's Will. Will we lay down our lives daily so that God can save the world? Is our conditional submission enough? "I protest by your rejoicing which I have in Christ Jesus our Lord, I die daily." (1 Corinthians 15:31)

Jesus laid himself down in the grave and rose again so that we could taste the power of His resurrection.

> "That I may know him, and the power of his resurrection, and the fellowship of his sufferings, being made conformable unto his death;" (Philippians 3:10)

He wants us to lay down *our* lives daily so that He can resurrect His Spirit *through* us and save His people from destruction. God *knows* our needs and desires; He tells *us* not to worry about them.

> "Therefore take no thought, saying, What shall we eat? or, What shall we drink? or, Wherewithal shall we be clothed? (For after these things do the Gentiles seek:) for your heavenly Father knoweth that ye have need of all things. (Matthew 6:31-32)

We must die to our worries, fears, unbalanced emotions, wounds, lusts and be resurrected to joy, peace, love, kindness, longsuffering, and faith. We must make the choice to die so that others might see Jesus in us and glorify the Father. No matter what the circumstances, if it is raining or the sun is out, our daily death, burial and the Spirit's resurrection from "self" allows God to live in our hearts. Our children are changed and even *look* different in the presence of God. Our relationships are new and fresh.

Everyday is a new beginning, allowing us to rediscover every aspect of our lives. The "baggage" we have been carrying everyday has been lifted off of our shoulders and we can be free to experience newness. Through the presence of God in our lives, our pasts are dead and our futures are bright. Our lives are no longer a burden to us and we are freed to live carefree in the presence of God. "And the work of righteousness shall be peace; and the effect of righteousness quietness and assurance for ever. And my people shall dwell in a peaceable habitation, and in sure dwellings, and in quiet resting places;" (Isaiah 32:17-18)

When we are humbly submitting to change, our lives are in daily subjection to the Holy Spirit. We are not swayed by the situations that arise during the day, for we are strengthened when we endure every circumstance, good *or* bad. Through our circumstances, we can identify with the lost, for *we* have been lost. We can relate to the poor and downtrodden, for *we* have experienced an intense famine in *our* lives. We can connect with the sick and afflicted, for *our* bodies have endured many afflictions to obtain the fulfillment of God's Word in our lives. Regardless of what we have – whether it is *five* dollars or *two hundred thousand* dollars in our bank accounts – our focus is not swayed by what we *have*, but only by *who* we have. Naturally, we think that the more money we have, the harder it would be to *give* money, but *true* faith is tested when we have many needs of our own and we *still* give the little that we do have in our obedience to God.

Our lives are not burdened by the conformity that success and suffering brings. We are liberated to seek God and His righteousness without any thought of self preservation. We are fixated on intimately communing with God through the sincerity of our hearts to be *shaped by His breath, moved by His touch* and *transformed by His words*.

Encampment #17

CANAAN

"Speak unto the children of Israel,.….When ye are passed over Jordan into the land of Canaan; Then ye shall drive out all the inhabitants of the land from before you,..…..for I have given you the land to possess it.

Numbers 33:51-53

A Life of Ministry

"All the commandments which I command thee this day shall ye observe to do, that ye may live, and multiply, and go in and possess the land which the LORD sware unto your fathers. And thou shalt remember all the way which the LORD thy God led thee these forty years in the wilderness, to humble thee, and to prove thee, to know what was in thine heart, whether thou wouldest keep his commandments, or no. For the LORD thy God bringeth thee into a good land, a land of brooks of water, of fountains and depths that spring out of valleys and hills; A land of wheat, and barley, and vines, and fig trees, and pomegranates; a land of oil olive, and honey; A land wherein thou shalt eat bread without scarceness, thou shalt not lack any thing in it; a land whose stones are iron, and out of whose hills thou mayest dig brass. When thou hast eaten and art full, then thou shalt bless the LORD thy God for the good land which he hath given thee." (Deuteronomy 8:1-2, 7-10)

After enduring the wilderness, we receive clarity of our divine purpose in God; nevertheless, we *still* have to walk into our destiny. God has equipped us with wisdom and knowledge of Him. He has refined our hearts into His image and clothed us with His righteousness. We have endured many temptations of the devil and we have been filled with love to effectively serve His people. God has connected us to the *right* people and we have been divinely placed into our positions.

We can not minimize the importance what God did for us in the wilderness, but it is vital that we never take our eyes off of God; we must stay focused on our tasks ahead. The wilderness is the journey God takes us *through*, that He can use us and empower us; it is not our *resting* place. Yet, we can not forget the way of which we were taught in the wilderness or we will fall into serving our *ministry*, not serving God.

> "Beware that thou forget not the LORD thy God, in not keeping his commandments, and his judgments, and his statutes, which I command thee this day: Lest when thou hast eaten and art full, and hast built goodly houses, and dwelt therein; And when thy herds and thy flocks multiply, and thy silver and thy gold is multiplied, and all that thou hast is multiplied; Then thine heart be lifted up, and thou forget the LORD thy God, which brought thee forth out of the land of Egypt, from the house of bondage; Who led thee through that great and terrible wilderness, wherein were fiery serpents, and scorpions, and drought, where there was no water; who brought thee forth water out of the rock of flint; Who fed thee in the wilderness with manna, which thy fathers knew not, that he might humble thee, and that he might prove thee, to do thee good at thy latter end; And thou say in thine heart, My power and the might of mine hand hath gotten me this wealth. But thou shalt remember the LORD thy God: for it is he that giveth thee power to get wealth, that he may establish his covenant which he sware unto thy fathers, as it is this day." (Deuteronomy 8:11-18)

We must remember the journey that has empowered us to a greater understanding of God and use what we have learned to empower others to know God more intimately and fulfill their divine purpose. We all want the power to gain wealth but it is through the wilderness that we gain this power. Our relationship with God is true prosperity, material wealth can not compare to what we have gained through our experiences in the wilderness.

The wilderness is our rite of passage for the divine place that God has set for us to rest in. Our purpose in ministry is not to build *our* kingdom and have people bound to serving *us*; our focus is to *serve*, by meeting the needs of the *people* with the gifts He has placed in our hands. Our gifts and positions should never be used to exalt ourselves in the presence of men, but to exalt *God* before men. Our service is to enlighten men of the heavenly treasures that God has in store for those who will surrender to His will. Our ministry is to draw the lost or misguided back to the knowledge of God. God wants to manifest His presence through our service to His people, but if He is not glorified then our ministries are in vain.

It is necessary for us to be receptive and attentive to the call of God and never get stuck in our comfortable routines because *our* ways will lead us to destruction and unfruitfulness. *God's* ways will humble, instruct and empower us to maintain our passion for the presence of God. For that reason, we must never skip our daily devotions in the presence of God; for it is through our time with *Him*, that our lives are refreshed and our energies are renewed. "Not by works of righteousness which we have done, but according to his mercy he saved us, by the washing of regeneration, and renewing of the Holy Ghost;" (Titus 3:5)

Our alone time with Him keeps us focused on His plan and quench the fire of self ambition. Our role is not to fulfill *our* carnal dreams, but to *fulfill* His divine purpose in us. If you are a writer, submit your gift to God and let Him write *through* you. If you are a singer, let Him sing *through* you. *Whatever* your gift is, let *God* use you, for our efforts will always be unfruitful to His kingdom. When we ignore the call of God in our lives, we dry out the wells of water that God has placed in us to quench the thirst of His people.

When we try to sustain our ministry in our own strength, it will lead us back to wandering in a dry and thirsty land. We must realize our thirst and the thirst of God's people can only be satisfied by the rivers of God. "... Jesus stood and cried, saying, If any man thirst, let him come unto me, and drink. He that believeth on me, as the scripture hath said, out of his belly shall flow rivers of living water." (John 7:37-38) When we are rooted in God, no matter what the devil brings to tempt us, we understand that our thirst only is quenched by the presence of God.

Our ministry is to embrace the lost and to stir up the gift of God that is in them. This world is *full* of lost sheep looking and searching for direction. They have searched high and low for something or someone that they can identify with. Who is pleading the case for God? We have journeyed through the wilderness, and now we must make our ministries the instrument that penetrates the hearts of the lost and bring God's people back into His presence.

> "And an highway shall be there, and a way, and it shall be called The way of holiness; the unclean shall not pass over it; but it shall be for those: the wayfaring men, though fools, shall not err therein. No lion shall be there, nor any ravenous

Humbly Submitting to Change

beast shall go up thereon, it shall not be found there; but the redeemed shall walk there:" (Isaiah 35:8-9)

God is ready to redeem and He is ready to deliver the sheep that are hungry for change in their lives. They have been wandering for too long on their own and God wants to use us to reconnect them back with Him. We *know* the way to God, so we must cry out to all the lost and hungry sheep, so they can meet God in the midst of *their* wilderness experience.

God wants to breathe life to the dryness in the lives of His people. He desires to fill the desert place with flowing rivers of His spirit. It is through His streams that flow in our lives, that we will be able to satisfy the needs of His sheep. "And the LORD shall guide thee continually, and satisfy thy soul in drought, and make fat thy bones: and thou shalt be like a watered garden, and like a spring of water, whose waters fail not." (Isaiah 58:11) He is calling for us to gather and feed His sheep. *Will we yield our lives so they may eat and live?*

About the Author

E'yen Gardner is a naturally gifted writer. Since the time of his elementary school days, God has given E'yen the ability to express himself through writing. E'yen has been recognized for his talent with recognition awards, published poetry and the love of his family and peers, by simply sharing his personal testimonies.

E'yen has a strong passion to spread the gospel of Jesus Christ to everyone. His passion is extended through many areas, one of which he is the chief writer for, *Step Into Fold*, a daily blog that bares his transparency and love for God's people (view at: www.myspace.com/stepintofold). E'yen co-teaches the Young Adult Class for the Sunday School Department, and is a Youth Leader for Teens at his church home, and is also the Owner and Senior Writer for Printed Word Publishing (PWP) company.

E'yen is a supportive husband to his wife and "crown" of 9 years, Maia Gardner, and is an active and devoted father to all five of his children. E'yen and Maia are currently waiting the arrival of their sixth child, expected in the Summer of 2009.

E'yen loves to write, dance, and teach. Some of his hobbies include playing sports, running, spending time with his wife and children, reading and watching movies.

Printed in the United States
220625BV00003B/6/P